JOHNNY COBB: CONFEDERATE ARISTOCRAT

UNIVERSITY OF GEORGIA MONOGRAPHS NO. 11

Johnny Cobb:
Confederate
Aristocrat

By

HORACE MONTGOMERY

DEPARTMENT OF HISTORY
UNIVERSITY OF GEORGIA

UNIVERSITY OF GEORGIA PRESS

ATHENS   1964

To

TOM

Contents

Preface

THE generation to which John A. Cobb belonged was much too young to wrestle with the momentous problems confronting the American people during the decade of the 1850's. Many of its members were destined, however, to march to war once their fathers decided early in the next decade to remit those issues to the sword. Young Cobb promptly joined the Confederate forces, taking with him to Virginia in April 1861 pleasant memories of Lucy Barrow, a teen-ager back in Athens, Georgia, whom he had known since childhood. Johnny and Lucy were soon exchanging letters, and in a short time a casual friendship blossomed into a genuine love affair. After the Confederacy's ill-fated Maryland campaign of September 1862, Johnny was given permission to leave the army and return to Georgia. For the remainder of the war he was in charge of the numerous Cobb plantations in the central and southwestern parts of the state. During the summer of 1863 he and Lucy were married, but the circumstances of war were such as frequently to keep them apart, sometimes for weeks without interruption. During the periods of their separation, before and after marriage, they corresponded freely, recording, along with their routine experiences, their fondest hopes and most frightening fears. Many of those letters have been preserved and were generously used in the preparation of this work.

Although there has never been a full-blown aristocracy in the United States, yet several incipient patriciates have existed at various times in our history. The affluent folks of the ante-bellum South fit this category, and both Johnny Cobb and Lucy Barrow, who belonged to this social group, recorded the ordeals through which it passed on its way to extinction during the war years. Here then is a close-up view of a Confederate aristocratic family: how its men performed under battle conditions; how it responded to news from the front; how it sought to preserve itself, at times forsaking its noblesse oblige; and how finally it behaved during its hour of deepest humiliation.

While this is a story loaded with pathos, it has a lighter side. There are moments of jollity. Lucy was a charming youth. She had a delightful sense of humor and strong feelings about individual responsibility. Often she was able to make the most of these traits and rescue both her husband and herself from trying circumstances. Late in the war, while Johnny was looking after the plantations, Lucy in the best aristocratic tradition gave her time and talents to looking after the Confederate soldier. As the operator of an embryonic "USO," she met many troopers. Of some of them she recorded her impressions, as both she and Johnny did of folks generally. Around these impressions much of this book has been written.

Numerous persons and agencies have rendered valuable assistance in the preparation of this work. To Dr. Kenneth Coleman, my colleague in the History Department at the University of Georgia, I wish to express my thanks for his numerous helpful suggestions. I am especially indebted to Lucy Taylor Bucknell of Bluemont, Virginia. A granddaughter of Johnny and Lucy, she has an abiding interest in the Cobbs and Barrows and was kind enough to let me use many family letters in her possession. Will Erwin and Howell Erwin, Jr., both of Athens, Georgia, have been equally generous and to them I am deeply in debt for the privilege of using many Cobb family letters. To John W. Bonner, Jr., and Susan B. Tate, of the Special Collections Division of the University of Georgia Library, I express my appreciation for generously placing at my disposal their time and talents; and to the Social Science Research Council of the University of Georgia and Dean Robert McRorie, the University's Director of Research, I am grateful for making certain funds available to defray some of the costs incidental to the preparation of this work.

Horace Montgomery

History Department
University of Georgia

JOHN (JOHNNY) ADDISON COBB

MRS. JOHN ADDISON COBB
(NEE LUCY BARROW)

HOWELL COBB, SR.

MRS. HOWELL COBB, SR.

Chapter I

Johnny Goes to War

AFFECTIONATELY known as Johnny, John Addison Cobb of Athens, Georgia, was twenty-two years old when in January of 1861 his state seceded from the Union. His father was Howell Cobb, who during the preceding month had resigned from President James Buchanan's cabinet. After leaving Washington, the elder Cobb took an active part in Georgia's secession and then became a leading figure in the founding of the Confederacy. Johnny's uncle was John B. Lamar of Macon. For twenty years "Uncle John," a bachelor, had managed his own and the Cobb plantations located in Jefferson, Baldwin, Bibb, and Sumter counties. In 1859 Johnny went to live with his uncle, helping to care for seven plantations and eight hundred slaves.[1]

Young Cobb's apprenticeship was, however, soon to be interrupted by war. Like his younger brothers, Lamar and Howell, Jr., he planned to join one of the Georgia infantry units being formed to fight the Yankees. Early in March of 1861 Johnny's father, shortly to conclude his duties as presiding officer of the convention in Montgomery, Alabama, which was organizing the Southern Confederacy, wrote him that if Virginia seceded Rebel armies could capture Washington and occupy the White House in a matter of months.[2] Cheered by the optimism of his father and anxious to return to the city where as the son of a Federal official he had frequently lived, young Cobb enlisted as a private in Company B, Second Battalion, Georgia Infantry. On April 20 he and his brother Lamar, also a private, left Macon with this company bound for Sewall Point, a short distance north of Norfolk and across Hampton Roads from the Yankee-held Fort Monroe. The

Cobb boys were thus among the first Confederate troops to reach Virginia, arriving a few days after that state had seceded.[3]

At Sewall Point Johnny and his brother were introduced to camp life. It consisted of breakfast at 7:00 A.M., roll call an hour later, and company drill until noon. Then came the mid-day meal, which was followed by several hours of free time. At 5:00 P.M. there was the battalion parade. Next came the evening meal, some more free time, and finally taps. Sleeping accommodations were the simplest. Each man had a cotton bag filled with hay. This he placed on several inches of straw which had been scattered upon the ground. Covering consisted of a gray blanket and an enamel cloth. Although primitive, such bedding was superior to the bare ground. After a month Johnny complained that his unit had come to be known as the "Marching Battalion." He hoped General P. G. T. Beauregard would soon take over as commander of Confederate forces in Virginia. Marching and everything else connected with a Rebel's military life would then be aimed at finding the enemy and thrashing him soundly.[4]

One week after he arrived in Virginia, Johnny requested his uncle to send him a Negro servant named Phil. The slave was to bring along his musical instruments, among them a fife, to enliven the camp's social life. Once Phil arrived, he quickly added his bit. He fiddled at evening dances attended by young ladies from Norfolk. He bought food from the local residents and served the five-man mess to which the Cobb boys belonged a substantial fare of salt pork, sausage, fried fish, middling beans, Rio coffee, and hot biscuits.[5] Johnny and Lamar were popular with their mess mates.

Both were in Virginia in response to what they understood as the Southern ideal of freedom. Their father was a planter-politician. Like many of his contemporaries, he was part democrat and part aristocrat. The Cobb boys were thus of the affluent class, a fact they made no effort to conceal from their comrades. Johnny was proud, independent, and opinionated. At times he was as stubborn as a plantation mule. Although usually well restrained, he could be fussy, was often given to grumbling, and on occasions succumbed to fits of anger. With the proper motivation he could swear adequately, if not eloquently. Lamar was quite the opposite. He was modest and pious, and like his mother, Mary Ann, very religious. He fell in love quickly and completely, professing his feelings not only to his sweetheart, but to his mother and father as well.[6]

Despite the constant tramping required by exacting drill masters and the large number of mosquitoes and ticks which assailed the tender ankles of Rebel soldiers, the Cobb boys would seem to have adjusted pretty well to camp life on Virginia soil. Johnny, however, promptly developed a strong aversion for tidewater Virginians. Shortly after his arrival in camp, he wrote his mother that they were the "most worthless set of people I ever saw." He believed them utterly incapable of helping themselves. He and his fellow Georgians, who had come to assist them, were regarded as a mere collection of hirelings. To fight for such a people did not offer a pleasant prospect for the young Georgian. "I have," he explained to his mother on May 3, "a contempt for Virginians . . . they had better go back into the Union for they are not fit associates for high minded people." To his uncle he wrote later that the Virginians "are the meanest set of people it was ever [my] luck to get among."[7] Toward these Johnny-come-lately Rebels of Virginia's tidewater, Cobb's feelings were strangely similar to those which a century later were to inspire in so many places throughout the world the scornful exhortation "Yankee go home."

Perhaps the enlisted man has ever ascribed to local civilians and to his own officers a diabolical talent to irritate the common soldier. Two and one half months after reaching Virginia, Johnny Cobb complained to his uncle that it was "very fine to make a reputation by going to the wars in the ranks, but the thing don't pay, particularly when you see men getting into good positions who are too lazy and good for nothing to start as a private."[8] Young Cobb and his Rebel mates quickly discovered an effective way to get even with their superiors. "Spanking Officers" was the designation given this interesting diversion. About thirty men would organize themselves into a company, send a squad after an officer, and "have him brought out and spanked with sword." Johnny boasted that nearly every officer of the battalion was subjected to this treatment. "So you see," he pointed out, "we are not under as strict military rule as some would suppose." Jestingly, he concluded: "Would it not be a pretty sight for Old Abe and his crowd to have witnessed?"[9]

Although the Cobb boys got along well with their mates, Johnny was bitterly disappointed that the Second Georgia Battalion refused to vote itself into the regiment his father was organizing during the summer of 1861. Known as the Sixteenth Georgia Regiment, the last two of its ten companies had by mid-August arrived at the Richmond Fair Grounds. Here, about one mile from the State House, Camp Cobb was established, and here the regiment remained until October 19. By early August the two Cobb boys had transferred from the battalion at Sewall Point to their father's staff, Johnny as quartermaster sergeant and Lamar as sergeant major. Soon after their transfer, both went home. Before the end of August they were back in camp, each bringing a horse and Lamar leaving behind a young bride.[10]

Colonel Howell Cobb slept in camp and during the day attended sessions of the Provisional Congress, then meeting in Richmond. Until August 31, when the lawmakers over whom he presided adjourned, the Sixteenth Regiment was in charge of Lieutenant Colonel Goode Bryan, a veteran of the Mexican War. Bryan sometimes called on the Cobb boys to help with drilling, each on at least one occasion taking half a company because the captain was indisposed and his lieutenants, in the words of Johnny, were either ill or successfully pretended to be so. Although he was now on his father's staff, John A. Cobb could find no charms about soldiering. He considered some of his duties downright onerous. Pay days were the most trying. They were like "paying off negroes their cotton money." The men had the greatest difficulty in understanding what was coming to them. A third were unable to write their names, while half of those who undertook to do so produced the most inelegant signatures.[11]

There were other annoying experiences for Johnny at Camp Cobb. Early in September the Sixteenth Regiment was ordered to report to General John B. Magruder's "Army of the Peninsula," whose headquarters was near Yorktown.[12] Magruder had graduated from West Point in 1830 and had

served as an artillery officer during the Mexican War. On
April 20, 1861, when he resigned from the Federal army,
he was in the rank of brevet lieutenant colonel. Early in the
war he was put in charge of the Confederate forces on the
lower Peninsula. He promptly distinguished himself as an
organizer, soon rising to the rank of major general.[13] The
Cobbs were anxious to join "Prince John," as the general was
known. Johnny fully expected the regiment to leave Camp
Cobb around mid-September. It did not get away, however,
until October 19.

Sickness was partly to blame for the month's delay. At one
time three hundred men were laid up with "chills and violent
intermittent fevers." The chills and fevers were caused by
epidemics of measles and mumps. Facilities for taking care of
the sick were meager, and some of the men left camp in search
of the greater comforts of Richmond homes. Many were un-
acquainted with the rudiments of personal hygiene, one of
them, according to Johnny, taking "a bath under a pump while
the fever was on him. . . ." By the time it was two months
old and weeks before it was armed, the Sixteenth had lost
thirty men to disease. Difficulties in getting arms further post-
poned the departure from Camp Cobb. Not until mid-October
did a consignment of Enfield rifles arrive in Richmond. When
they were broken open and inspected, they proved to be rusty.
Another four or five days were lost.[14]

Colonel Cobb made good use of the extended stay at the
Richmond Fair Grounds. With Congress now adjourned, he
settled down to learn the essential duties of a field officer.
He poured over Hardee's *Tactics*;[15] he listened carefully to
the instructions of both Lieutenant Colonel Bryan and Adjutant James Barrow; [16] and by mid-October he had progressed
far enough to shout regimental commands from horseback.[17]
Thus had a successful Southern politician, whose experiences
had been limited to the law and public service, moved into
the military hierarchy of the newly formed Confederacy.

Early on October 19 the men of the Sixteenth Georgia
Regiment left Camp Cobb for good. Climbing aboard the cars
of the Richmond and York River Railroad, they rode off to
West Point. Here they embarked on the C.S.S. *Logan* for
Yorktown. By nightfall they had reached this historic Virginia

town, marched a half mile farther downstream, and there amidst some small cedars spent the night on the wet ground. The next morning saw them pushing on another three miles to the site of their new home, which, in honor of their second in command, they named Camp Bryan. The Sixteenth's new camp was located in the middle of a clover field which was surrounded by a forest containing nuts, grapes, and wild turkeys. Situated near the Yorktown-Newport News Road in the vicinity of Grafton Church, Camp Bryan turned out to be temporary.[18]

Johnny's regiment was now part of General Magruder's "Army of the Peninsula." Its assignment was to watch the Federal force at Fort Monroe. Work was therefore begun at once on the construction of fortifications about one mile to the south of the new camp. The elder Cobb and Magruder were in daily conference and quickly became close friends.[19] The Cobbs, of whom there were now four on the Peninsula, all developed a fondness for "Prince John."[20] He had a flair for histrionics, exclaiming after hearing of the Confederate victory at Leesburg that thereafter the great command must be: "There is the enemy—destroy him." Johnny believed Magruder planned to use the Sixteenth as a "flying regiment," seeking out the enemy, striking him, and then fleeing.[21]

Life on the Peninsula during the first winter of the war was dull for Quartermaster Sergeant Cobb. Unhappy with his duties from the start, he was now complaining about the endless paper work demanded by Richmond. "After my twelve months is out," he wrote his Uncle John on December 16, "the wealth of the Rothschilds would not induce me to remain in the Q. M. dept." A sense of duty to his father, he continued, was the sole reason he did not immediately return to the ranks as a private. Frightfully cold weather compounded the young Georgian's woes. Although Camp Bryan's tents were equipped with chimneys, they were uncomfortable, Johnny recording early in January that he had "slept warm" only one night in two weeks. As for his father's regiment, when not on false runs after Yankees, it was engaged in building fortifications and constructing winter quarters.[22]

Letters from home did not always boost Johnny's morale. His mother wrote early in December that Uncle Tom

(T. R. R.) Cobb, on furlough from the Peninsula, had pictured a dark future before a crowd of Athenians gathered in the Presbyterian Church. Without friends, the Confederacy had only God to rely upon. Mrs. Cobb thought Tom's speech had alarmed the women and encouraged old Unionists to talk of reconstruction. At about the same time word of the Charleston fire reached the Peninsula.[23] Johnny suggested to his Uncle John that it could have been the work of "some of our Yankee friends, who are still among us." They should all be run out, he insisted, but, he added bitterly, that would be hard to do "when Jeff Davis is . . . giving them high military positions over the heads of our own countrymen. . . ." The elevation of Davis to the Presidency, he went on, was a mistake equalled only by the election of Joseph E. Brown as Georgia's governor.[24] When Johnny's furlough was suddenly cancelled just before Christmas, his anguish was heightened and his disenchantment seemed complete. A distraught son was hardly comforted by his mother's observation that the Confederacy's first Christmas was marred by an ungenerous Santa Claus. He had been forced, wrote she, to assume "a *neutral* position in imitation of the great European powers."[25] The new year brought a turn in Johnny's luck. He got his furlough and with it were to come happier days.

CHAPTER II

Johnny Chooses a Sweetheart

EARLY in 1862 Johnny took leave of Virginia, heading straight for Macon. There around the hearth of Uncle John B. Lamar he joined his mother and the younger Cobb children, then in Macon for their customary winter visit. Before the war the Bear's Den, as the bachelor uncle often referred to his abode, had become a second home for Johnny. Ensconced there in mid-winter, young Cobb was far removed from the annoying details of military life in Virginia. He must have been relieved to be in Macon, enjoying the luxury that only a soldier on furlough appreciates. Yet his heart was not really at the Bear's Den. It had taken flight one hundred miles northward to Athens. Near Athens lived Lucy Pope Barrow, daughter of David Crenshaw and Sara Pope Barrow. When Lucy was ten her mother died. Thereafter Grandma Pope and Priscilla F. Sawyer, a governess from New England, directed the lives and attended the wants of Lucy and her eight brothers and sisters.[1]

Lucy was now seventeen and she was pretty. Already the elegance of her manners was attracting attention, a tribute to both Miss Sawyer and Lucy Cobb Institute in Athens.[2] The Barrows and Cobbs had long been acquainted, the older Cobb boys and Lucy since childhood. On February 2, 1862, John Cobb made a momentous decision. With characteristic directness, he wrote asking Lucy to marry him.[3] Was his affection for her "reciprocated"? he asked.[4] He must have known how Lucy felt about him, for almost a year earlier she had written Lamar that she liked Johnny "best, and simply because I think he likes me best."[5]

Pleased with the young soldier's show of attention, Lucy nevertheless withheld her answer for what must have seemed

8

to both youngsters an eternity. During the long delay she showed Johnny's letter to her brother James, who at Lucy's request gave timely assistance to this incipient affair of the heart. Not more than two days after Lucy received the letter of proposal James wrote Johnny to explain his sister's behavior. Lucy, he pointed out, was "yet a school girl" and she wished to confer with her father before replying. After making it clear that his sister would have preferred writing herself, James concluded his short letter by suggesting that Johnny might expedite matters by returning to Virginia via Athens.[6] Finally on February 25, about three weeks after receiving the proposal from Johnny, Lucy composed her answer. Without her father's sanction, she explained, "I did not feel at liberty to express my sentiments." Assuring young Cobb that his feelings for her were "fully and sincerely" returned in kind, she gleefully reported that her father would "appose no obstacle to the successful issue" of her suitor's wishes.

Satisfied that his courtship was off to a good start, Johnny returned directly to Richmond early in March. Meanwhile, he had been commissioned a captain and made aid-de-camp to his father, himself advanced to brigadier general and placed in command of the newly formed Second Brigade. It was composed of Cobb's old Sixteenth Regiment, his brother Tom's Georgia Legion, the Twenty-fourth Georgia Regiment, the Fifteenth North Carolina Regiment, and the Second Louisiana Regiment. Brigadier General Cobb was promptly ordered to take his command of some 5,000 men to Goldsboro, North Carolina. There he was to protect two important railroads running south from Richmond from a Federal force already in possession of New Bern, Morehead City, and other North Carolina seacoast towns. On the way Johnny complained that he had been in the service almost a year and had yet to get within three miles of a Yankee. He hoped his luck would change once he reached Goldsboro, but there he was to find no Yankees either. Not only was the scarcity of Yankees bothering Johnny, good country butter was also hard to find. But the remedy for this was simpler. He could and did appeal to his mother.[7]

Early in April the Second Brigade was ordered to Virginia. A disappointed Johnny followed a few days later with horses and baggage, bitterly observing that he had hoped never again to return to the Peninsula.[8] Upon reaching Virginia, the Second Brigade was again attached to Magruder's forces, which on April 12 became a part of General Joseph E. Johnston's command. To stop Union General George B. McClellan's thrust up the Peninsula from Fort Monroe, Magruder placed his troops along the western bank of the Warwick River.[9] It was a small stream rising a short distance from Yorktown and flowing southward across the Peninsula to the James River. As a part of Brigadier General McLaws' Division, the Second Brigade was stationed along the Yorktown-Warwick Line at a place called Lee's Mill. For about a week Cobb's men stared across the Warwick at the Yankees. On April 16 a hot fight occurred, lasting for three hours. Cobb reported his losses had not exceeded 20 killed and 70 wounded. The Georgia butter which Johnny prized so highly probably never reached him, but he had met his first Yankees. According to his father, young Cobb had been "as cool as a cucumber."[10]

For over two weeks after the fight at Lee's Mill the Second Brigade was in some hastily constructed trenches along the Warwick River. Johnny thought the Yankees had quieted down because they were convinced the Rebel position was strong. Yet their guns worked both day and night. The weather was cold and wet, and fires were forbidden. Even so, Johnny reported that he was living well. Coffee and biscuits were plentiful, and on occasion there was an "old rooster" for supper.[11]

It was at this time that Brigadier General Cobb's good friend Magruder was having his trouble with the Confederate high command. In mid-April he was reduced to a division commander. Among the units assigned to him was Cobb's Second Brigade. Early in May it was ordered to fall back toward Richmond. By the end of the month Johnston's entire army of 50,000 had withdrawn to within a few miles of the Rebel capital in anticipation of McClellan's assault on that city. The Second Brigade's position was on the southern bank of the Chickahominy River, about four miles from Richmond and equidistant below the Mechanicsville Bridge. Here Johnny again found himself looking across a river at Bluecoats.

Again Rebs and Yanks were awaiting the battle both knew was soon to come.[12]

Early in June Johnny explained that for days he had intended writing, but marching over bad roads up and down the southern bank of the Chickahominy had made it impossible. "We have had hard work marching around looking for a fight, but have not found it yet," he complained to Lucy on the 4th. The fight that was not "found" had already taken place on May 31-June 1 at Seven Pines. That Johnny was unaware of what had been happening around him was betrayed by his wish of June 4 that the "Yankees would hurry up and cross the Chickahominy if they intend to . . . and let us have the big fight . . . for I am getting tired of waiting on them [and] looking every day for a fight." Actually, McClellan's left had crossed the river below the Second Brigade's position for the engagement at Seven Pines and there it remained after the battle. However, directly across the river from Johnny was McClellan's right wing, the river thus dividing the Yankee forces.[13]

The early June days of 1862 were indeed discomfiting for Johnny. With Yankees in front of him and to the right of him, athwart the Chickahominy, he was complaining of fruitless marching to get into a "big fight." Nor was this all of his troubles. Meals had become most irregular, on one occasion the men of the Second Brigade going for an entire day without food. Worse still were the incessant rains and the almost knee-deep mud. Among Johnny's associates there was some speculation on the cause of the heavy downpours, one Reb advancing the theory that "the fire and punch of canon [sic]" somehow opened the heavens and released the rains. "Camp letter scrawl" was Johnny's apologetic description of his letter of June 4 to Lucy, adding that he had written little else than "special orders" for so long he almost forgot how to address a civilian. Nevertheless he hoped it worthy of a reply.

On Sunday, June 29 came Lucy's reply. Her mood was gloomy. She had not gone to church, because she was "ailin." Apologetically, she continued: "I expect you think my health must be very poor, for everytime you hear from me I am a *little* unwell." She promptly assured her lover that he need have no anxiety on her account. "I eat well, sleep well, look perfectly well, and generally feel perfectly well," she added. Her condition she described as "rest satisfied," and she observed that several persons had told her she never looked better. How Johnny would react to such self-esteem bothered Lucy. His pardon for her egotism would have been more formally sought, had she not flattered herself "with the belief that you like to hear *about* me as well as *from* me." That was her feeling with respect to him and she supposed "the same rule holds good in both cases." Lucy had gilded the masterly touch of feminine acquisitiveness with womankind's disarming gift of feigned innocence and weakness.

Johnny replied on July 6: "When you write always tell me how you are, for it certainly would detract from the pleasure it gives me to receive a letter from you if you said nothing about yourself." This was hardly the language of the committed, impetuous lover, who, perceiving his first duty as that of the comforter, composes repetitious boasts of his deep love and affection. But this was John Cobb writing to the girl he loved and was to marry. He readily cursed Virginians, Joe Brown, Jeff Davis, and certain Confederate generals. Lucy would doubtless have preferred that he turn some of his emotional steam toward love-making.

An awkwardness persisted in the courtship of John and Lucy by correspondence. Rather soon after it began she asked: ". . . do you like for me to call you by your name, or do you wish me to say Mr. Cobb, or Capt.?" Johnny was not to imagine that she wished a "formal Miss" to precede her name. Nothing, she assured her sweetheart, was further from her thoughts. He promptly registered an objection to such formality, for "it would sound too cold and distant." As Lucy had no desire to have her own name preceded "hereafter with a formal Miss," he could not imagine what had put the idea into her head. Yet with Johnny a cold formality was to continue, less apparent than real.[14]

Lucy had access to the avenues of local gossip, and she dutifully recorded some of it for Johnny. Her brother James, home to recover from a wound received at Lee's Mill was fond of Jule Toombs of Washington, in Wilkes County and about forty miles from Athens. Jule, however, was reported engaged to "a great blubbery, gawky" boy named Sam Hardeman. His hopes drooping, but with the advantage of a battle scar, James went to Washington to press his cause. He returned "full of bright hopes for the future," though Lucy admitted Jule had not completely forsaken Sam. Early summer of 1862 found wounded heroes and soldiers on furlough mingling with the low country folks who moved on Athens in great numbers. Hotels were full. The Franklin House had 120 boarders and even Lucy Cobb Institute was turned into a boarding house to care for people who had come from Savannah, Charleston, and New Orleans. Local citizens believed low country folks fair game for any tales their behavior might inspire. Some of the visitors were parties to pathetic events born of the war. Lucy was particularly distraught over the behavior of a woman from New Orleans. The mother of three little girls, the oldest ten and the youngest six, she left them at the Institute and went on to Richmond to join her husband, a major in a Louisiana regiment. For Lucy the sight of those "three little things so early alone in the world" was unforgettable. She heard the little one cry "as though her heart would break, calling piteously for Mother! Mother!" That mother, declared Lucy, should have stayed with her children; her husband was able to care for himself.[15]

Meanwhile, Johnny was participating in the final stages of the Peninsular Campaign. This ill-starred undertaking ended on July 1 with the brisk encounter at Malvern Hill, the last engagement of the Seven Days' Battle, June 25-July 1. Cobb's Second Brigade saw stiff action at this point, Johnny writing Lucy that it had been the war's hardest and most desperate fight. Casualties were heavy, the Second Brigade losing about one-third of the 1500 men sent into battle. Federal losses were even greater and the Yankees, declared young Cobb, "are now retreating down the river as fast as they can." He assured Lucy that "a few more hard fights and . . . this war will be over, and then I will come home to stay . . . for I am tired of the war."[16]

For Johnny Malvern Hill was not without its amusing side. His own brother Howell and Lucy's brother Tom had, he wrote his fiancée on July 4, become very excited during the fight, young Barrow going so far as to give General Ma-

gruder some advice on troop movements. The fiery commander exploded with "By G___, lead them in," whereupon
Tom Barrow took the Second Georgia Regiment into the
fray. In recounting the battle to Lucy, Johnny remembered
that their brothers "were charging about and giving orders
as if they were in command of the army." Brother Lamar
also got into the act. "Old Magruder" called on him to make
a speech to one of the regiments exhibiting a noticeable
timidity. The young man performed nobly, declared his
brother, shouting exhortations above the din of battle.

John Cobb's amusement was not shared by the folks back
home. Disappointed Georgians were grumbling instead. Mrs.
Howell Cobb, whose husband and three sons had been at
Malvern Hill, was saddened by the gossip that was going the
rounds in Athens. "The whole story," she wrote her husband
on July 13, "is that Gen. Magruder, Gen. Toombs, and Gen.
Cobb were *drunk* upon the battlefield." A few editors assailed
the generals for their behavior during the battles around
Richmond, one ascribing McClellan's escape to their alleged
intoxication.[17]

The Peninsular Campaign left its mark on Johnny's father.
Unaccustomed to the demands on a field officer, the elder
Cobb became ill early in July. He went to Richmond to rest,
and finally on July 12 was granted a thirty-day furlough.
The exact nature of Cobb's malady is not certain. It is known,
however, that he complained of stomach pains and nervous-
ness. He had experienced several narrow escapes at Malvern
Hill, his son recounting one of them for Lucy. The hammer
of a gun which was lying on the ground a short distance from
Cobb was struck by "grape shot," sending a bullet within
inches of him. Reflection on this and other incidents of the
battle, the heavy losses of his brigade, and the charge back
home of "drunken generals" must have weighed heavily on
the sensitive disposition of this man. Long habituated to re-
solving civilian difficulties, Howell Cobb was finding military
duty extremely frustrating. Shortly before mid-July the
distressed general turned homeward. With him were his son
Johnny and Tom Barrow. On the way the elder man took a
turn for the worse. Upon reaching Augusta, it was decided to
remain there long enough for him to get back some of his

strength. On July 17 the unpleasant journey from Richmond to Athens was completed.[18]

The elder Cobb's strength returned quickly. In the meantime, his son enjoyed the opportunity to be with friends and relatives. He was regularly seen with Lucy. Soon it was rumored that they were to be married before Johnny returned to Virginia. To his Uncle John B. Lamar he confided that those who expected an early marriage were to be disappointed, regrettably observing that the only trouble with a furlough was "that it can't last."[19]

CHAPTER III

The Cruel War

ALTHOUGH Lucy Barrow was only sixteen years old when the Civil War began, she quickly acquired the anxieties commonly held by her elders. In Virginia with Johnny Cobb were her three oldest brothers.[1] All four Athenians were in Brigadier General Cobb's Second Brigade. Not until the engagement at Lee's Mill on April 16, 1862, was the brigade in a real fight. Consequently, during the first year of the war Lucy's brothers, her sweetheart, and many of her friends were in no great danger. Nonetheless, this sensitive girl had become acutely aware of the meaning of war and could write about it in appropriate cadence. On the anniversary of the firing on Fort Sumter she recorded her impressions under the title "The Horrors of War."[2] Like her elders, Lucy believed Southern whites were struggling for "liberty and human rights." The awful price was the war's horrors. Throughout the Confederacy this was the all-absorbing topic of interest and conversation. "Hearts once gay and free as the lark," were now overwhelmed with bitterness and sorrow. Yet this, she hastened to add, was preferable to the enslavement of Southern white people by Yankees. Many a bright spirit had suddenly become "as cold and silent as the shadow of death." She hoped none was indifferent to "those dear ones" who had willingly resigned "home, friends, the comforts and enjoyments of life to battle for us and our country."

How wide was the circulation of Lucy's "Horrors" is not known. Hardly a model composition, it was a fair expression of the sentiments of Southern womanhood. Devotion, sadness, and bitterness all vied for primacy in the soul of this youthful girl. Yet Lucy was not the prisoner of the pessimistic fatalism that abounds in her account of April 12, 1862. Indeed, her letters to Johnny, at this time and for long afterwards, disclose a refreshing sense of humor. As her brothers unwillingly returned to far away Virginia at the close of their furloughs, she could record such light-hearted doggerel as:

> Tis mighty hard to go,
> But if so be's I must,
> I follows after him
> As goes hisself the fust.[3]

On August 17 Johnny and his father were back with the Second Brigade. They found it encamped near the James River ten or twelve miles below Richmond. The next morning both men were up early reviewing the troops. They had scarcely begun when Major General LaFayette McLaws joined them. McLaws had graduated from West Point in 1842. His Mexican War record was less distinguished than that of Magruder. During the Peninsular Campaign he performed brilliantly as a division commander. As a tactician he was sound, but he was excitable and at times given to indulgence in extravagant and abusive language, an impropriety of which Cobb was later to become an unfortunate victim.[4] On the morning of August 18, McLaws and the two Cobbs rode off in search of McClellan, who, Johnny observed, "is doing something but what it is no one knows." About nine o'clock that evening the Cobbs were back in camp, convinced the Union commander had "skedaddled." A long letter to Lucy ended Johnny's busy day. He vowed he would not get up in the morning "at day light as the order calls for," but instead would sleep late and for this privilege willingly forego his breakfast.[5]

The month that followed Johnny's return to Virginia was to be a momentous time both for him and for his country's cause. For the Confederacy it was to bring the failure of the Maryland invasion. For Johnny it was to be a time of great sorrow over the death of his beloved Uncle John in the Maryland battles. Despite his rapid movements during these days, Johnny managed to write Lucy regularly. Always he provided interesting details about the life of the Rebel

soldier, but never was he the impetuous lover. Although Lucy
rarely complained about young Cobb's self-restraint, she preferred the bold professions of a lover for his darling to
descriptions of the minutiae of military life.

General McClellan's "skedaddling" of mid-August had
resulted from his being ordered back to the Potomac River to
reinforce General John Pope, who had decided to move against
Richmond by the overland route.[6] Meanwhile, General Lee
had turned the main body of his army northward to prevent the Union commander from realizing his objective. A
few days after Brigadier General Cobb and his son returned
from Georgia, the Second Brigade, still in McLaws' Division, was ordered to join the main Confederate forces under
Robert E. Lee, commanding general since June 1.[7] Accordingly, its wagons, horses, and men were loaded on railroad
cars at Richmond. Johnny reported that in checking to see
whether his horse was properly loaded, he had placed his
valise against a fence. Returning a few minutes later, he
could not find it. A search in the darkness would have been
useless. Overcome with anger, Johnny confessed to abusing
"Virginians and everything connected with them" before
his "good humor" was restored.[8]

By August 21 Cobb's men were encamped about one mile
from Hanover Junction. Complaining that it had taken nearly
nine hours to make this trip of approximately thirty miles,
Johnny related that both he and his father had slept on the
ground during their first night at the Junction. From ten
o'clock until daybreak it had rained steadily. A single blanket
had been Johnny's only protection. On August 23 John B.
Lamar and Howell, Jr., arrived on horseback from Richmond
to join the Second Brigade staff. When Howell, Jr., brought
out his package of letters from home it was to contain none
from Lucy, Johnny writing her that evening of his disappointment and confessing that he was "getting spoiled," looking
for a letter too often.

Lucy had a reason for not writing. She had gone to Madison
Springs without pen or ink, having forgotten them in the
"hustle and bustle" of leaving home. Thus two weeks were
to pass "without one line to explain whether or not such
neglect was intentional."[9] Twenty-three miles northwest of

Athens, Madison Springs was advertised during the late 'fifties as "This Garden Spot of Georgia." Its waters were publicized as "impregnated with iron," and efficacious in the cure of numerous diseases. Early in the war its announcement boasted that it could not be surpassed for climate, health, beauty, waters, and scenery, "and in fact everything that can delight the eye or taste."[10] On one of his furloughs Johnny had spent a few days there. The Athenians he had encountered disgusted him. He thought all of them "toadies," particularly in the presence of Savannah people. Like Virginians, Savannahians infuriated Johnny. He hoped that Lucy's party included some worthy Athenians, with enough "independence to cut them."[11]

Lucy enjoyed her two weeks at the Springs, admitting, however, to negligence in drinking the mineral water. The result was that she returned home "in about as poor looks" as when she had left. Declaring it impossible for her "to get fat," she vowed her determination to stop trying. Among the pleasures at Madison Springs had been a "Fancy Ball." It was an impromptu affair, with nearly everybody taking part. Johnny's brother Lamar attended as "King of the Cannibal Isles." Dressed in a gay costume of "red-blue gilt and black," his was a distinct appearance. His young wife took the part of Queen Anne Boleyn, "gorgeously arrayed in blue silk and black velvet." Upon being introduced to the King of the Isles, one of the guests, apparently impersonating the celebrated Lady Dorothy Pakington, demanded: "Of what ile, castor ile or sweet ile?" "Of all iles," was the King's reply. "La," countered Lady Pakington, "What a greasy man you must be!" The ubiquitous John Bull was also present. With a silver snuff box, he was able to exude his normal complement of "pompous civility" by insisting his admirers take "frequent pinches" of its contents.[12]

In concluding her observations on the Madison Springs jollities, Lucy's mood became one of guilt. "You may wonder," she wrote Johnny, "how such gaities can find tolerance in these troublous times." Had the ball been a "studied affair," she confessed she would have been uneasy. But it had been merely a way of spending one evening. She could not believe such pleasures "wrong and sinful," but she admitted "some painful twinges of conscience for seeking so earnestly for enjoyment when those so dear to me were far away—perhaps lonely—homesick and sad—while I—but the thought chokes me—I cannot—will not—give it utterance."[13]

Madison Springs, Georgia, was a long way from Hanover Junction, Virginia. From the latter place John Cobb reported on August 24 the presence of some 12,000 Rebel troops. Major General D. H. Hill, commanding his own and McLaws' divisions, was awaiting the order to race forward to join Lee, now moving rapidly toward the Maryland border. The following day the fateful order came. At once the Second Brigade's Negroes began preparing three days of rations. On the twenty-eighth Johnny was sixty miles farther north, at Rapidan Station. It had been a hard march and he accused Hill of sheer brutality. Employing such terms as "mean," "hard hearted," and "contemptible," the Georgia soldier claimed the general had conducted the march without "any regard whatever for the men." Many of the Second Brigade's men suffered from exhaustion, one dying along the roadside. Hundreds complained of sore feet and would have to be left behind. Young Cobb claimed Hill aspired to the image of another "Stonewall" Jackson, whose brother-in-law he was.[14]

Like many of his fellow officers, Hill had served in the Mexican War. In 1849 he had resigned his captaincy in the army for a professorship at Washington College in Lexington, Virginia. From 1854 to 1859 he held a similar position at Davidson College in North Carolina. Thereafter he became superintendent of the North Carolina Military Institute in Charlotte. At the opening of the Civil War he was made a colonel of the First North Carolina Regiment. As a division commander he distinguished himself during the Peninsular Campaign. At the time of the Maryland invasion he held the rank of major general.[15] Hill's illustrious feats on the Peninsula did not impress John Cobb. Instead he belabored the starchy general for having refused to accept impulsive Robert Toombs' challenge to a duel. An altercation between the two men during the Battle of Malvern Hill had brought forth the summons.[16] Young Cobb opined that Toombs would surely have killed Hill. Both the army and the Confederacy would have profited from his death and Toombs would have had the distinction of adding "another recruit to the muster roll of h____."[17]

On August 28 Johnny reported between 20,000 and 25,000 troops at Rapidan Station. The next day Hill was to start his divisions toward Culpeper, about twenty miles to the north. Where he would take them from there, Johnny did not know. He hoped they would not catch up with the Yankees, or ever hear of them again for that matter. Johnny's earlier notion about the glamor of war had completely vanished. As he pondered what lay ahead, his thoughts kept returning to Hill, the callous commander who seemed bent upon driving his charges until they fell over from exhaustion. Everywhere the young Georgian heard grumbling. Even the elder Cobb joined in denouncing the "inhuman" march from Hanover Junction. If he had to remain under Hill much longer, Johnny confided to Lucy, he would desert, return to Georgia, and submit to conscription. Desertion and conscription together would be less degrading than being under Hill. As if Johnny's marching troubles were not enough, Lucy's letters had suddenly stopped. She was at Madison Springs, and had written but one letter since young Cobb left home weeks earlier. He feared he would "wear that out reading it" before another reached him.[18]

From Culpeper Major General D. H. Hill led his own division and that of McLaws to within a few miles of Leesburg, Virginia, just south of the Potomac River. There McLaws' men promptly bivouacked, the Second Brigade naming its camp after Johnny's sister Sarah. Johnny was proud of his father's brigade, boasting it was the best in the Confederate service. To prove his claim, he cited its behavior immediately after encampment. While other brigades were tearing down fences to make fires, the Second refused to touch a rail until its commander gave the order. Young Cobb thought "men had to be well disciplined to stand and see others violate orders and not do it themselves." Because the men knew he would not "make them do anything he does not think . . . right," his father was cheerfully obeyed. Always, observed the son, their comfort was the elder Cobb's first concern. Johnny's comforts, however, went beyond those of the ordinary foot-soldier. He had made the latter part of the trip from Richmond in the saddle. It had saved his feet and improved his disposition to the point where he was now even referring to General Hill in deferential tones. Still greater conveniences in travel were being plannd with his Uncle John B. Lamar. They were "going to war in a buggy," driving Uncle John's horse one day and his own Nelly the next.[19]

Bivouacked in the rich farming area of northern Virginia, the Rebels, observed Johnny, were finding "everything in the eating line . . . bountiful and cheap." The region had suffered very little from fighting. Indeed, it was prospering from the war, discovering in the Federal capital a greedy market for its surplus. Northern Virginians proved to be less offensive to Johnny than the people around Richmond and on the Peninsula. If not polite, they were at least agreeable, the· women waving their handkerchiefs as a gesture of friendship. The Georgian presumed they had shown the same courtesy to four hundred Yankee horsemen who had recently been in Leesburg.[20]

Arriving at Camp Sarah on September 3, Johnny wrote Lucy two letters the following day and another on the 5th. In each he recorded his impressions of the Second Bull Run battlefield, over which he had passed on the way to Leesburg. Never had he seen "anything the equal of the dead of the Yankees—a great deal larger than ours." He thought they must have fought well, "for the field is covered with their dead." Confederate losses, Lucy was assured, were "nothing like theirs." Many of "ours were wounded," admitted cobb, but "most of them very slightly." The roads around Bull Run's battlefield were choked with Rebels who had been in the late battle. Johnny talked with some of them, observing that "a great many . . . had one finger shot off." Buck Green, who had suffered a leg wound and was hobbling along on a crutch, told Johnny that of the twenty-seven men in his company, twenty-six were shot down but only "a few" were killed.[21]

That the Yankees had been badly whipped at Second Bull Run Johnny had not the slightest doubt. He was convinced they would never again make "the same obstinate resistance." Though himself still weary of the war, observing that if he ever got home again he would stay there, Johnny's despair and resentment of recent days had become less evident. What he saw at Bull Run had become a profound experience. It gave the Georgian new hope; yet it was a hope inseparable from despair and anguish. It also gave him a sense of purpose and a contempt for the enemy. A little fighting and a lot of fast running, he wrote, had ever been specialties of the Yankees. Had they not "skedaddled" from the Peninsula and then suffered a rout at Bull Run? Small wonder Rebel hopes in general and Johnny's in particular were now high. The moment for boldness had arrived, and Confederate leaders were preparing to strike. If successful, Johnny believed the war would be over in about sixty days. He would write again "when we take Washington," though he admitted he might find it more suitable to wait until he reached Baltimore or Philadelphia.[22]

From Camp Sarah, Johnny registered his old complaint to Lucy for her failure to write more often. His own letters continued the pattern of reporting the experiences of a Rebel on the march. In none of them did he indicate in the slightest that there was any chance of his succumbing to lovemaking through the mails. There were, however, two important differences between them and most of his earlier letters. As observed, they were weighted with a new *élan vital*. They also reveal that Johnny was torn between the need for security of military information and the desire to relate to his sweetheart what he understood as the unfolding drama of troop movements and forthcoming encounters with the enemy. After observing on September 4 that a great Confederate force was rendezvousing near Leesburg, he wrote that he could say nothing further about "our force here or about our movements as we are in a position that our letters run the risk of falling into the hands of the enemy." Forgetting his precautions of September 4, Johnny recorded the next day that A. P. Hill, "Stonewall" Jackson, and James Longstreet were all to move their commands into Maryland by September 6. As for the Second Brigade, it was making preparations to move across the river momentarily. Still unborn was the twentieth century notion of military security.[23]

About the time the Second Brigade was crossing the Potomac and heading toward Frederick, Maryland, Lucy confessed to Johnny that she had "not been doing as I have been done by as far as writing was concerned." She would make it

up with an extraordinarily long letter in which for the first
time she mentioned matrimony. Johnny should have heard,
wrote she, a discussion on this subject between Grandma Pope
and his grandfather, the senior John A. Cobb. That part of the
exchange which had struck Lucy's fancy was her grandmother's bold declaration that girls should marry while young.
To this the elder Cobb retorted by professing his admiration
for "old maids." Grandmother Pope had made her point and
won the argument, thought Lucy, but there was some question whether Grandfather Cobb had been convinced. Lucy
too was on the side of young brides, and hopeful enough
to believe the elder Cobb's namesake would see to it that she
did not join the old maids, for to him she now explained that
he must take her for what she was—very innocent and often
behaving with a "want of sense." For example, she had forsaken her studies at Lucy Cobb Institute, because she was
getting "stupefied." Doubting the wisdom of this action, she
began "studying a little," borrowing from the Franklin College
Library a three-volume work on Old English. According to
Johnny's mother, Lucy was determined to read the books
because President Moses Waddel of the College had expressed
the opinion that she was incapable of understanding their contents.[24]

When she visited at the Barrow home on September 8,
Mrs. Howell Cobb found Lucy "bright and shiny." Like
many Athenians, both Johnny's mother and his sweetheart
were elated over the "glorious victory" at the Second Battle
of Bull Run. Lucy was especially optimistic, certain that
Washington had fallen when the train whistled "so loud and
long" on the evening of September 6. To learn the next day
that the blowing had been caused by a stubborn cow which
had wandered onto the tracks was, of course, a disappointment,
but one which lost some of its sting because it was also amusing. Her Johnny would yet make it to Washington and
Baltimore, perhaps even to Philadelphia and New York. While
she could not be with him, he was to do the next best thing
and take a lock of her hair along. Procurement was solved
with the aid of his sister Mary Ann, who wrapped some
braided ringlets in a thin blue paper marked, "This is Lucy's
hair." On September 8, Johnny's mother dispatched the small

packet, observing, in a letter of this date, that while she did not comprehend its meaning it doubtless fulfilled "some request of yours." If so, Johnny had begun to show signs of giving in to that inner compulsion Lucy instinctively knew would one day come to her aid.

Lucy was pleased with Johnny's two letters of September 4 from Leesburg, writing on the 18th that for six days she had been sick and was then "sitting up in bed to scribble you a little letter." In Athens and everywhere, she reported, there was much sickness and death. Scarcely a family had not lost a relative or friend. Saddest of all was the case of Tom Billups. While walking in his sleep on a train of cars, he stepped off the rear platform to become the third member of his family to die within a year. Lucy supposed Johnny was in Maryland, and she wondered how the people there were receiving the soldiers soon to enter "as victors into Washington."[25] Little did she know about the events that had taken place since Johnny's letters from Leesburg. She had not yet learned of the mighty battles at Crampton's Gap and Antietam, which were to deny Johnny a hero's entrance into Washington and send him to Georgia stricken with grief instead.

On September 9 General Lee in faraway Maryland made the risky decision to divide his army, one part to advance to Hagerstown and the other to oust the Union force at Harpers Ferry. Between the Confederate army and its double objective lay South Mountain, extending northward from the Potomac River across Maryland and into Pennsylvania. The region beyond the mountain was accessible through numerous passes. Closing them, to prevent Union forces to the east of Frederick from hitting the Confederate rear, became one of McLaws' duties. To Howell Cobb was given the task of helping to plug Crampton's Gap, where on the afternoon of September 14, Colonel Thomas T. Munford reported excessive pressure. McLaws urged Cobb to hasten to the gap and hold it, "if it costs the life of every man in [your] command."[26]

Cobb immediately ordered two of his regiments to the gap, and personally took two more. Ascending the mountain amidst great disorder, he managed to reach the top. Below, on the eastern slope, he saw the defending force's flanks under heavy attack. He promptly threw his four regiments into the fight, two on either flank. With the flanks braced, the enemy suddenly slammed himself against the center with such force as to break the Confederate line. Colonel Munford reported that Cobb's men turned and raced to the gap's top, fleeing down the western slope like ". . . a flock of frightened sheep."[27] An unlettered private had a slightly different version of what happened to these men: "Old Cob runn them down a mountain rite into the Yankies, then ordered them to retreat. When it was almost impossible, they had to crawl up the mountain and the Yankies shooting them like squirls."[28] Second Brigade losses in killed and wounded numbered between 300 and 500.[29]

Among those killed was Colonel John B. Lamar, who fell while near his commander's side and died the next day from excessive loss of blood.[30] Johnny and his brother Howell, Jr., accompanied their uncle's body to Macon.[31] Lamar's death was a cruel blow to the entire Cobb family. Especially grieved was Johnny, long a close companion of the master of the Bear's Den. He wrote Lucy on October 8 that it would have been so much easier on all, had he been taken instead of his beloved uncle. "I would have been missed I know," he admitted, "but my place could have been easily filled for I have never been of much importance to myself or anyone else."

Johnny was not to return to the Army of Northern Virginia. His father became embroiled in a bitter altercation with McLaws, who during the hectic events of September 14 and after, had accused Cobb of failure to understand his responsibility. On September 24 Cobb, complaining of his senior's abusive language, requested an immediate transfer.[32] The elder Cobb wished to be closer home. Now that Uncle John was dead, Cobb's family and finances needed his attention. He hoped to have Johnny released from the army to manage the plantations in middle and southwest Georgia and his own command moved to Georgia.[33]

En route to Macon with his uncle's body, Johnny stopped in Richmond long enough to confer with Colonel William M. Browne, aid-de-camp of President Davis, about a transfer for his father.[34] About a month later Howell, returning home on furlough, also called on his friend Browne and discussed with him the detachment of the Second Brigade from the

Army of Northern Virginia.[35] A few days before reaching
Athens on October 29, Cobb himself was ordered to report
to General P. G. T. Beauregard, then Commandant at Charleston, South Carolina.[36] At once Howell began negotiations
with Richmond authorities to have his oldest son detailed to
direct the overseers of the Cobb plantations.[37] Although ap-
proval took months, Johnny promptly settled down to perform the duties learned as an apprentice of his Uncle John.[38]

CHAPTER IV

Master of the Bear's Den

ALONE in the Bear's Den a few days after his uncle's burial, Johnny had time for reflection. For the first time since the awful contest at Crampton's Gap, he now realized Uncle John was dead. Everything around him, he wrote Lucy on October 8, recalled happier days. It would be the same when he visited the plantations in Sumter, Worth, Bibb, and Baldwin counties. He had been with Uncle John "as much there as here and . . . talked with him about everything connected with the management of the different places." Johnny would go to Americus and then on to the plantations in Sumter and Worth counties as soon as Phil returned from Augusta, where he had gone for young Cobb's horse. Once Johnny left for the plantations in southwest Georgia, Lucy must not expect to hear from him. There was but a single post office in the area of the plantations. This he believed a better excuse than "the one about having 'no ink.' "[1]

Johnny had misgivings about his new assignment. To his brother he confided that he would have preferred staying in Virginia with the "fighting army," but someone had to manage the plantations and "I had just as well be put to trouble as anyone else."[2] It was "dull business," he wrote Lucy, "staying here in this big house by myself. . . ." For breakfast, "Old Davy" served him coffee, corn bread, butter, and broiled bacon; at midday, tea was substituted for coffee; and for dinner, bacon greens, butter beans, corn bread, and sweet potatoes. With flour selling at from forty to one hundred dollars a barrel, biscuits had become only a memory. It was the same with milk. Johnny often thought about the war; however, since leaving Virginia his information was usually

28

out of date or based on the wildest rumors. But the weather, like his loneliness and what he ate, was a subject on which he had first-hand information. October was hot and dry in Macon, he wrote; and, he observed, if ever he had any energy, the weather had taken it all away. He confessed to never feeling "as lazy in my life."[3]

While Lucy's sweetheart was now ensconced in the Bear's Den, her three older brothers were still in Virginia. Tom, the youngest of them, was winning a reputation for industry and bravery. Lucy was proud of him, but could not help wondering if he would be spared. While others were suffering anguish and distress, why was she so richly blessed? *"None* taken! *All* left!" This was the glorious hope to be entertained; but she often thought it would be well to prepare to meet the shock of death, *"if* it should come." On the other hand, she wondered if to contemplate for any length of time the loss of friends and brothers would really lighten the news of death. She concluded that it would not, adding that because of her optimistic nature "I don't find it a hard matter."[4]

Lucy's three younger brothers were her immediate concern. To them she often acted as a nursemaid. They were a lively set, even wild, Lucy thought, on rainy Sundays. Such days taxed her resources; she would offer them books, apples and chestnuts, usually to no avail. The threat of sending them to bed worked sometimes. Of the three, Dave, who was to become chancellor of the University of Georgia, was the most mischievous. When Miss Sawyer, the faithful governess, handed him *The Forest Exiles,* he looked at it and exclaimed: "La! Miss Sawyer—dat aint no Sunday book! de old bad man'll git me! Umph! I believe Miss Sawyer'd rather I'd go to de bad place den to make a little fuss!"[5]

Soon after John A. Cobb returned to Georgia, Lucy found herself writing him on a rainy Sunday afternoon in October. What a doleful day it must have been for him, she conjectured. She fancied him alone in dusky quarters, lounging on a couch, his eyes lidded and his face wan. Rousing himself, he drowsily called for lights and food. She imagined him then walking to a window and swearing at the weather, returning to the supper table and growling over the fare for a while, and finally wishing he were in Athens. She too wished he were in Athens and assured him of her "sincerest sympathy" in the loneliness she fancied had overwhelmed him. But Johnny had not spent this day as Lucy imagined. He had instead found pleasant employment for his time, writing her and his mother.[6]

John Cobb's horse turned out to be a big disappointment. His uncle had paid $500 for her and it cost Johnny over $100 to get her out of Virginia. The first time he hitched her to a buggy, she promptly began showing the bottoms of her hind feet. "Not liking that kind of fun," young Cobb was afoot again and forced to delay his departure for southwest Georgia until October 18.[7] He found the Sumter and Worth plantations in satisfactory condition. At the former he spent one day chatting with overseer Stancil Barwick, nicknamed by Howell, Jr., Ransy Sniffle from his resemblance to that dirt-eating character in A. B. Longstreet's *Georgia Scenes*. At each of the plantations he had a "glorious time . . . chewing sugar cane," a delicacy he would have enjoyed sharing with Lucy's three little brothers. He would visit the plantations in Bibb and Baldwin counties, and then come to Athens.[8]

Back at the Bear's Den after a ten-day absence, Johnny resumed his grumbling about the loneliness there. More than ever, he wished he could be in Athens. Of his plight, Lucy had not been unaware. As observed, Johnny had scarcely settled down in Macon when she put her fertile imagination to work, commiserating with her lover whose solitude she fancied unbearable. That Johnny was showing signs of comprehending the mating instinct must have been comforting to Lucy. Soon after his return from southwest Georgia, he wrote: "How a boy can love a girl who does not love him, I don't see." He could not, nor would he ever, be a party to such an arrangement, boasting that he was strong enough to "conquer that."[9]

Life in Macon contrasted sharply to soldiering in Virginia and Maryland. Johnny believed those at home suffered more than their friends and relatives in the army, for in the army there was always something exciting to draw a man's mind away from danger, hardship, and home. Johnny had tried both, "and as far as a choice of places goes I had rather be with the army." He had no intention of returning to the army, however. At home he would remain, unless Georgia was "invaded," a forbidding but likely prospect. Troops would be needed to defend the state before the winter was over, thought Johnny, and he hoped the rumor that the Second Brigade was to draw this assignment would prove true. "We would feel almost as if our friends were at home if they [Second Brigade] were in Georgia."[10]

Johnny had been out of the army only a short time when he discovered how the war had changed the old way of living. For him, one of the most distasteful developments was the rise of a class of speculators. He believed they were responsible for the high prices of so many necessities. In Sumter and Worth counties he knew many poor women who wanted to make uniforms for the men in Virginia, but could not afford to pay the prices for yarn and wool. These and many other badly needed articles were being held off the market in Macon to force up prices. Young Cobb believed the government should put down the speculators and seize the materials it needed to conduct the war. He claimed the speculators were protesting loudly against the farmers for trying to raise the price of corn. While not condoning this practice of farmers, Johnny believed agricultural folks were forced to employ the speculators' tactics as a means of self-protection.[11]

By early November 1862 it had been confirmed that the Second Brigade was to be sent south. Most of Brigadier General Cobb's staff was to come along; at least, so rumor had it. Both Lucy and Johnny rejoiced at the news, but, as so often with such news, Lucy after brief reflection wrote her sweetheart that she hardly knew "whether to be glad or sorry that you all are coming to Georgia." She feared it would turn out to be a move from "quiet winter quarters to a hot fierce winter campaign." All her reservations melted before the prospect of Johnny's return to Athens within a week.[12]

The Cobbs, except Tom, and two of Lucy's three older brothers, were back in Georgia by mid-November of 1862. Brigadier General Cobb was preparing to take care of them. His first duty, however, was to put his business interests in order. As Johnny was already in charge of the plantations in middle and southwest Georgia, this problem was well on the road to solution. With assurance that the Second Brigade was soon to come south, the elder Cobb was in a favorable position to look after his two sons, Lamar and Howell, Jr., and the three Barrow boys. Thus it was that in mid-November 1862, Athens was to become a mecca for Cobbs, Barrows, and their friends. Here the elder Cobb's plans were to take final form, and arrangements to carry them out were perfected.[13]

Such was the situation when Johnny took his first leave of Macon. During his short visit in Athens there were parties and teas; pleasant evenings were spent playing cards, backgammon, and blindman's buff; there was dancing; and there was also serious planning for an uncertain future. Amidst the merriment and gravity, the new master of the Bear's Den found time to pay active court to Lucy Barrow.[14]

Late in November Johnny and Lucy's brother Pope left for Macon, making part of the trip by train and stopping for the night at Milledgeville. There they spent a pleasant evening with friends, going on to Macon the next forenoon. A day later Johnny's father and brother Lamar joined them. Soon all but Johnny would depart for Florida, where the elder Cobb, with the aid of his Second Brigade, was to begin his duties as Commandant of the newly-formed Military District of Middle Florida. Of this Johnny hated to think, because, as he wrote Lucy, "I will be more lonesome than I was before, for then I had begun to get used to it."[15]

Johnny's return to the Bear's Den left Lucy in low spirits. Her plans for a "Regular romping country frolic" with friends were spoiled, when both she and her grandmother were stricken with mumps. Early December found her "literally down in the mouth," particularly at meal times. As she sat down to write Johnny on December 7, her gas light failed. Left in total darkness, she was about to give up when Grandma Pope entered her room with a tallow candle. Beginning her letter in a mood of gloom, Lucy explained that the Barrow household had changed greatly since Johnny's visit. Father Barrow was now rarely at home, doing his patriotic duty by setting up salt works in Florida and vigorously working his plantations. "Nobody here but Grandma's Cousin Jule and myself, except indeed the little children . . . we are three old cronies, grumbling and complaining about everything in general—and the 'mumps' in particular." She would give anything to see another face in the family circle, "somebody who would advance a few new ideas and give a new impulse to our stagnant life." When Johnny's mother, calling to see the afflicted, reported that Colonel William Browne would shortly be her house guest and that she was expecting Johnny to entertain him, Lucy begged, "You can come, can't you Johnny? I am so lonely, and want to see you so much . . . ." Covered with gutters and burning dimly, Lucy's candle urged a "goodnight" and "ever your own."[16]

Although Johnny seems not to have been in Athens in December, Lucy and her brother Pope spent part of the holidays in Macon. Lucy visited the Bear's Den, which she thought was a pleasant place "to lounge in," and with Johnny called on friends. At the "Christmas tree" party Johnny became so ill he had to leave. Unable to return until it was nearly over, he was mortified by the thought that some might think he had been under the influence of liquor. He was certain Lucy knew better, for they had been together all day and, he explained, he was as sober "as I ever was in my life."[17]

Soon after her return to Athens, Lucy was treated to a rare sight. Busy with a party at Dr. Moore's on January 4, she went to bed late and awakened the next morning to behold a beautiful snowfall. Promptly venturing into it with thin shoes, her feet got wet and cold. While warming them before the fire, she wrote Johnny and watched excited Athenians hurl snowballs at each other. Grandma Pope, apparently recovered from the mumps, was as enthusiastic as the youngsters, joining cousins, fat men, and thin ones in snowballing and sleigh riding. "Oh! what fun we are having," wrote Lucy, wishing Johnny and her brothers were in the Classic City to frolic with her.

Lucy's "snowy letter" did not reach Johnny for a month. The mails were slow and besides Johnny was visiting the plantations. In Milledgeville he found time to attend some parties. When he returned to Macon for a few days before leaving for the southwest, his Uncle John Cobb and Lucy's brother James paid him short visits. The latter was on his way from Richmond to Quincy, Florida, Howell Cobb's headquarters. He had gone to the Confederate capital to get per-

mission for "the Genl.," as Johnny now referred to his
father, to raise troops in his new district. Permission was granted, and the troops were to have the same status as others in
the Confederate service. Also, James had conferred with the
Secretary of War about Tom Barrow's transfer to Florida.
This transfer would have to be approved by General Lee,
but since the Confederate commander would do "anything
reasonable that the Genl. will ask," Johnny was confident of
Tom's transfer.[18]

Johnny spent the last days of January and the first week
of February looking after plantation affairs in southwest
Georgia. From Sumter County he wrote Lucy a "birthday
letter" on February 1. It was Sunday. The next day would
be Lucy's birthday. It would also be the anniversary of his
first letter to her. He recalled that on his birthday she had
observed that a birthday was the proper time for "sober
thoughts and reflection," a time "to ask oneself what good
they [sic] had done during the year." He had tried to follow
her rule, but confessed he gave up because he could think of
nothing he had done that really mattered. With Lucy, he
continued, it was different. He was certain that once she had
reflected upon all she had done during the past year, she
could not say that she had "lived for nothing." He could
tell her one thing she had done. Perhaps it did not matter to
any one else, but to him it had been of "great importance,"
and "as I think you take some interest in my welfare I will
tell you."[19]

If Lucy expected the confessions of an ardent lover, she
was to be disappointed. The best Johnny could do was to
pay his respects to the "great benefit" of her "influence over
me for the last year." He then vaguely alluded to "a great
many things that I would have done if I had been left to
myself." Thereupon he abruptly left the subject by claiming
he had already written enough about himself.[20]

Johnny was back in Macon by February 10, busy getting
his plantation records in shape. Expecting to leave for Athens
in a few days, he hoped to spend at least a week there. Although no record has been found of a visit he may have made
to Athens in February of 1863, it is likely that he was there
between February 11 and 21. At any rate, he was back

at the Bear's Den by the latter date. At that time he wrote his mother of a report he received in Macon that Confederate authorities were planning to seize 28,000 pounds of meat from the Sumter plantation. Young Cobb was unhappy over the prospect of giving up so much meat at the government price of 35¢ per pound. Late in the month he set out for Florida to confer with his father. Upon reaching Quincy, he found "the Genl." absent. Thereupon he rode over thirty miles through "lonesome . . . looking country" to Alum Bluff searching for him. At the Bluff he waited, "the Genl. & staff" arriving the next day. The two Cobbs discussed the Confederacy's food problem, the father expressing complete satisfaction with the policy of commandeering meat at 35¢ a pound.[21]

Johnny wrote Lucy about the wonders of Quincy. It was an attractive place, more comfortable at this time of year than "up the country." He observed that his father's staff was well acquainted with the ladies of the town, showing a decided preference for the widows. In young Cobb's opinion service in Florida was very different from what he had known in Virginia. It was, he believed, "more like a holiday here than work," with everybody having a much easier time than he was having staying alone in Macon. Johnny could report good news about Lucy's brother Tom. Friends who had recently seen him reported that he was well, and, equally as important, "the Genl." had written Richmond a letter which "he thinks will get Tom's transfer." For Lucy's grandmother there was also good news. Johnny had found her some mild "smoking tobacco" and he would send it shortly.[22]

John A. Cobb expected to be on a rigid self-imposed schedule during March. Late on the third he was to leave Quincy for Sumter County. There he would take time to arrange for the delivery to the government of over 22,000 pounds of meat. He would then go to Macon for a week or two and thereafter return to Quincy.[23]

CHAPTER V

"I Thee Wed"

FOR the Cobb family, March was to be the saddest time of the entire war. To be sure, there had been other times of sorrow. The previous September had been one of them. Then the beloved Uncle John B. Lamar had died of a wound received at Crampton's Gap. On December 13, Thomas R. R. Cobb was killed at the Battle of Fredericksburg. Both deaths had been shocking to all the Cobbs, particularly Mary Ann, wife of Howell. Having lost both her father and mother in childhood, she had come to look upon her brother John as a parent. As for Thomas R. R. Cobb, his piety had made him one of her favorites. For years she had held him up as an example to her husband, whose unorthodox religious views kept her in a constant state of uneasiness. Despondent for days at a time, Mrs. Cobb was in no condition to face the death in March of her infant son Tom. This blow fell with crushing force, plunging the already distraught mother into Stygian gloom. From it there seemed little hope of escape. Because Howell was confined to Florida, it was necessary for his three older sons to take turns staying with their mother in Athens. Johnny was to be unable to follow his neat schedule of appointments.[1]

On April 21 young Cobb returned to Macon from Athens. While at home helping to console his mother, he and Lucy had talked about their wedding. The day Johnny reached Macon he settled down in the Bear's Den, always loneliest just after a visit to Athens, and wrote to request her to set the date. He imposed the single condition that it be no later than the latter part of July.[2]

Thereupon the prospective groom confessed that his most

36

distinguishing trait had ever been self-restraint. Not only had
this denied him the role of the impetuous lover, but it had
also made difficult an expression of his true feeling for his
fiancée. However, he insisted, "if I do not love you as ardently
as a person can," then he admitted that he did not know the
meaning of love. Should Lucy doubt his true feeling for her,
he hoped some day to be able to convince her "that I speak
the truth."[3]

Lucy cheerfully agreed to a late July wedding, and, like
Johnny, preferred to invite a few guests to a private ceremony
at home. She did, however, request a pleasure tour of a few
weeks to Tallulah Falls and the north Georgia mountains, and
thus "avoid all those unpleasant congratulations and explana-
tions of surprise . . . ."[4] As her wedding day drew closer
Lucy had some misgivings. Might she not be too young and
childish to leave the "paternal roof" and take her place as the
wife of John A. Cobb. On May 30, two months before her
marriage, she urged him to "think well" before he made a
final decision. As for Johnny, he had clearly settled all doubts.
On that date he sent Lucy her engagement ring, hoping it
would remain an evidence of a contract that neither would
ever regret. In two months they were to be married, wrote
Johnny. He could hardly imagine it would ever be so. "Oh!
If only those two months were over!"[5]

Spellbound by her ring, Lucy boasted that she prized it
more highly than anything, "excepting the love which prompt-
ed the bestowal of it." Johnny might laugh and believe her the
victim of "fanciful nonsense," but, she eloquently protested,
"since I have the ring you seem much nearer and even dearer
than before." Always before, Johnny's presence in Athens
seemed like a passing vision and his "words like a sweet
whisper breathed into my ear in a dream of the night—something that left no trace behind—but now—no need to give
the full meaning of that word 'now'—enough that *now* I experience what is the *glorious reality*—and am happy in con-
sequence."[6]

All together, a prospective bride, a grieving mother, and
a government struggling to create a nation placed heavy re-
sponsibilities upon the youthful John A. Cobb. In April he
visited his mother and was disturbed at her extremely nervous

state. Even more upsetting to him was her preference for homeopathetic therapy. On the 11th he wrote his father to come home at once and urged him to take the ailing Mrs. Cobb back to Florida. After returning to Macon, he requested Lucy to keep him informed of his mother's condition.[7]

It will be recalled that Brigadier General Howell Cobb had approved the Confederacy's plan of commandeering planters' meat. Accordingly Johnny had delivered in early March 23,000 pounds of meat to the government at 35¢ per pound. At the same time he sent to Quincy 700 pounds of hams, a delicacy the elder Cobb regularly ordered.[8] Bacon and ham were now the most important staples of the Cobb plantations. Johnny traded them for much-needed shirting and sheeting, which he procured in 700-pound bales at the rate of one pound of bacon for one pound of cloth.[9]

With bacon and ham the key staples, cotton acreage had to be reduced or given up entirely. Early in 1863 Johnny and his father decided no cotton would be planted on any of their plantations.[10] Instead wheat, corn, oats, and ground peas were to be grown, and hogs would be turned into parts of these crops for fattening.[11]

Concluding one of his spring tours of the plantations, Johnny reported good crops of corn, wheat, and oats. He had sold a quantity of lard at 75¢ per pound, and was anxious to market four or five thousand bushels of corn. The Confederate government needed the corn to feed its mules and horses in middle Georgia, and was willing to pay $1.25 per bushel. However, it was without storage space and Johnny refused the use of his cribs for this purpose. In consequence, he had to plan to haul corn to market during the summer.[12]

Managing the widely scattered Cobb plantations in wartime was a trying assignment. With luck, a sizable sum of money could be realized from the sale of meat, corn, and wheat. Would this be enough to pay the running expenses? Johnny did not think so. Confederate taxes were high, so high in fact that he felt it necessary to sell over $3,000 worth of land in May of 1863 to help pay them. Even so, he could report a bank balance of only slightly over $10,000. Besides taxes, overseers' wages for the year would amount to at least $2,000. As overseers were hard to get, Johnny thought he should pay the Confederate tax on them.[13] The elder Cobb approved his son's judgment, bitterly observing that this tax was an outrage, "but," added the first president of the Confederacy's legislative body, "nothing better could be expected from such a set as the late Congress."[14] Taxes and overseers' wages were not to be the only expenditures. Over three hundred slaves would need shoes before winter and hundreds of bushels of salt would be necessary to preserve the meat that would begin to pile up with the coming of cold weather. As the Confederacy entered the third year of war, young Cobb faced a financial crisis, of which he was well aware. At this stage of the struggle he could have restored monetary balance to the family business simply by selling Confederate bonds. They were still valuable assets. But this was unthinkable to such devoted Confederates as the Cobbs.[15]

Although Johnny was busy during the two months before his wedding, he found life pretty dull. For relief, he read Sir Walter Scott's novels, attended at least one concert at Wesleyan College, and late in June made a quick trip to Athens.[16] On the way back to Macon he had a slight attack of cholera morbus, which he blamed on too "many mean cucumbers." Macon was hot during the summer of 1863, and after his Athens trip Johnny was gloomier than ever. "There is," he wrote Lucy on June 25, "very little pleasure in these short visits." A rash of fires in Macon did not help Johnny's disposition. The Brown House had one and on successive days the Lanier House was the victim. Young Cobb worked hard carrying furniture out of the Lanier House the second time it was on fire. Convinced that arsonists were responsible for these fires, which were all easily brought under control, Johnny asserted: "Old Lincoln has some of his emissaries at work among us."[17]

"I do wish that this war would come to an end, so that we can all be free agents again," lamented Johnny to his betrothed about one month before he took the wedding vows.[18] He yearned for the time when people could regulate their actions by their own desires and not the demands of conscript officers and "seizing agents." Within less than ten days he was to learn of the two Confederate disasters at Gettysburg and Vicksburg. Like many Georgians, Johnny could not understand the Vicksburg disaster. He thought it was strange that Lieutenant General John C. Pemberton should surrender because of starvation, when reports had led the people of the Confederacy to believe his provisions were sufficient to withstand a six-months' seige. In disgust he wrote Lucy on July 11, one week after Pemberton's surrender, "We are getting to be as big liars as the Yankees ever were." On the 16th he wrote his father that everything looked dark and gloomy. With General Braxton Bragg's Army of Tennessee, then encamped in Chattanooga, the only force between a rapidly growing Federal army in Tennessee and the southeast, Johnny wondered if Athens would long be safe. At the first sign of a raid south of the Tennessee border, his mother, still frequently confined to her bed "with nervous headache," and the children must be brought to Macon. Thus did young Cobb advise his father two weeks before he and Lucy were to be married. Perhaps the wedding would yet take place in the Bear's Den.[19]

Selecting a minister to perform the wedding ceremony proved momentarily embarrassing. Lucy objected to a Reverend Scott of Athens. He was, she opined, "rough—even uncouth in his manners," as well as dictatorial and conceited in dealing with his parishioners. She simply could not have him officiate "at this most important of all occasions." Would Johnny ask the Reverend Joseph S. Key of Macon to perform the ceremony?[20] On July 1, Johnny reported "the dread duty" performed. The Reverend Key would officiate.

One week later Lucy asked Johnny to move their wedding date ahead one day, to Wednesday, July 29. "To gratify your mother, to please myself and perhaps to vex you," was her way of bringing up the subject. Reminding Johnny that they both had originally wished to be married on that date, she hoped he would not be "overmuch vexed" at her request. That one had to deal "with a person of no persistency of purpose, no stability at all" was bad enough, but she pretended these to be constitutional weaknesses; and playfully warned, "if you have determined to take me—it must be covered with blemishes, just as I am."[21] Dutifully the bridegroom humbly carried out his betrothed's wish, and then proceeded to wind up all plantation business, so that by July 20 or 21 he could be in Athens to prepare for the termination of his bachelor-hood.[22]

On July 1 Johnny had written his father that he and Lucy were to be married on the 30th of the month, adding laconically: "I would like for you to be in Athens at the time if you can." So reticent had young Cobb been that ten days before the wedding he had not yet told Grandmother Cobb he was getting married. His mother complained that he and his betrothed had behaved like ostriches. It was her son's behavior, however, that had been most upsetting to the irate mother. He had imagined nobody knew what was going on, "when it turns out only *your kindred* knew nothing. . . ." Lucy's more numerous kin, on the other hand, knew all and told their friends everything "as a great secret." Acting for the humiliated Cobbs, Mary Ann ordered her son to begin forthwith to rectify matters by writing his grandmother.[23]

Lucy had misunderstood Mary Ann's reaction to changing the wedding date. Indeed, the elder woman had been annoyed by the change. Once convinced that it had been the work of Johnny, and that he had acted upon a "trivial pretext," she took the opportunity to upbraid him. Lucy would discover soon enough that "something of the tiger" lurked beneath Johnny's "lamb-like look." He must give his betrothed a glimpse of that beast and lessen the shock of post-nuptial discovery. Having made her point, Mary Ann assured Johnny he was now free to "paddle your own canoe," which, but for a wise mother, would long since have drifted away in the foul streams of "single stupidness." Herself wounded by the "tiger" of ingratitude and neglect, a mendicant mother concluded with the hope that her son would yet acquire a sense of duty "to the mother that bore you."[24]

No account of the wedding has been found in either the Cobb or Barrow correspondence. Only a terse notice appeared in the *Athens Southern Banner* of August 5, stating simply that on July 29 the young couple had been married by the Reverend Joseph S. Key at the home of the bride's father.[25] Elsewhere in this issue it was noted that on August 4 Howell had left Athens for Quincy, Florida. Apparently only their immediate families and friends witnessed Johnny and Lucy take the nuptial vows.

CHAPTER VI

"Why Must We Be Separated, Dear Johnny?"

FOR John Cobb and his lovely bride the bliss of honeymoon was soon over. Vacant for two weeks, the Bear's Den was calling for its master and he must return unattended. It was August and it was hot in Macon. To all who would inquire about his bride, the young husband gave a standard reply: it was simply too warm and uncomfortable to think of bringing her along. More than ever, Johnny missed Lucy. She was constantly in his thoughts. On the train from Athens he had dozed, his head falling on John Thomas' shoulder, and, he confessed, "I woke up thinking it was you and came very near kissing him before I found out where I was."[1]

Lucy's first hours of separation were also a time of heartache. Throughout the first day of their separation Johnny had not been out of mind for a single moment. But with the help of her sister Bly (Ella Patience), she got along "passably well" until night. Then, lamented the helpless bride of two weeks, "I missed you—oh! so much!" Lucy missed Johnny's "dear shoulder," the manly clasp of his arms, and his kind words and tender caresses. With so much earnestness and fervor she longed for him that it seemed as though her very heart had exhausted itself of longing. Unable to sleep or rest, she confessed to her husband that every thought of him "brought an additional toss and tumble." In desperation, she threw her arms about Bly, "thinking she was you," and "rubbed against her . . . back." Bly's patience worn out, she began "to grumble at me and the hot weather." Lucy slept little during this night and was fully awake at five-thirty with a "dull, listless feeling pervading every portion of her body." She could think only of the happy moments of the past two weeks and saw herself as a little child who had lost her dearest brother:

> His wings are grown
> He's flown—he's flown
> 'Cause I have none—I'm left [alone].

"Oh! Johnny why must we be separated? Why may we not enjoy life together?" From her confused world of happy memories, gnawing grief, and intense longing, Lucy returned to implore her darling not to forget the "pet names" when he wrote. She was yearning for them. Her own pet name for him she saved until the very end of her first letter; "God bless you, my darling old man!"[2]

Bad news awaited John Cobb upon his return to the Bear's Den. Governor Joe Brown was "after" his overseers and his Negroes.[3] It will be recalled that during the summer of 1863 the Cobbs had paid the Confederate government the exemption tax of $2,000 on their four overseers. Soon after the tax was paid Brown began to draft their overseers for state military service, snaring the fourth one while Johnny and Lucy were enjoying the first days of married life.[4] Brown, at this time running for re-election, was, in the opinion of Mary Ann Cobb, "making an argument for the votes of the poor" by instructing his agents "to exempt no one especially *overseers*." Johnny was no match for this "grand trickster," who, added Mrs. Cobb ironically, "may be one of God's elect and we don't know it."[5]

The day after he reached Macon, Johnny went to the state capital to see Colonel H. C. Wayne, Adjutant and Inspector General of Georgia, about the release of his overseers. Wayne proved unyielding, whereupon Johnny sought the advice of L. A. Whittle, his Macon attorney. Whittle advised that Cobb's difficulties with the state authorities be brought to the attention of Confederate Secretary of War James A. Seddon. The Macon lawyer believed Brown had no right to draft overseers and was confident Seddon would compel him to retract his order.[6]

On August 19 Brigadier General Howell Cobb wrote Seddon. He explained that the Confederate tax of $2,000 on his four overseers had been paid, and that subsequently Governor Brown drafted all of them for state military service. Cobb then proceeded to review his own contributions to the Confederate cause: he repeated that he had paid what the government required, so that his plantations might be cared for; he and his three sons were in the military service;[7] and he had abandoned cotton planting for raising food, which he was selling to the government at its own prices. Throwing himself on the mercy of the Confederate official, Cobb asserted that without immediate relief he would be ruined. Was he not entitled, he asked, to as much protection as those who were not in the service of their country? "Their overseers," he complained, "are detailed and not liable to Gov. Brown's call." As Cobb saw the problem, it was simply a case of Seddon overruling Brown by invoking the principle of equal protection of the law.

Should the Secretary of War fail the Cobbs, they were determined to test the issue in the courts, Johnny boasting that he was going to "see if Joe's legs cannot be knocked from under for once."[8] Seddon offered no relief and the matter was taken to court, the Georgia Supreme Court, from whose decision there could be no appeal, ruling some months later that such complainants as the Cobbs were without recourse.[9]

Here is a neat example of the conflict within the Confederacy between centralization and state rights. It is this conflict which has caused some historians to assert that the Confederacy could be born, but so strong was the attachment to state rights that it could not live. In their preoccupation with the problem of limiting the central power, the Confederate founders, of whom Cobb was a prominent one, would seem to have made possible the exercise of arbitrary power at the state level. Brown, whose talents are mindful of some twentieth century governors, scrupulously followed the popular line. Mary Ann Cobb was not entirely incorrect in ascribing to him a propensity for invoking a kind of class struggle. Brown's four terms as Georgia's chief executive suggest the extreme delicacy of constitutionalism when confronted with willful popular majorities.

At any rate, the Cobbs were no match for Joe Brown, with whom the war was soon to bring them in close, if not pleasant, relationship. Early in September Johnny slipped away from Macon for a short visit with his bride in Athens.[10] Returning on the 8th, he found "the Genl." at the Bear's Den en route to Atlanta. While in the latter city, the elder Cobb received orders from the Confederate War Department to remain there to organize the militia and other Georgia forces Brown had ordered to that city for duty in the Confederate cause.[11] Cobb must now return to Georgia; he must now work with General Bragg and Governor Brown. For Bragg, who, according to Johnny, would continue to be outflanked until the Yankees ran him into the Gulf of Mexico, Howell Cobb had little respect.[12] For Joe Brown he had only bitter contempt.

On his return to the Bear's Den on September 8 Johnny found, in addition to his father, a letter his wife had written weeks before, one in which she repeated her request for pet names. He promptly tried his skill, addressing his young bride as "My Dear Old Woman," wondering whether this was a satisfactory start, and finally closing with "Many kisses to the best old woman in the world."[13]

The next day young Cobb left for Sumter. For the first time since he had taken over the plantations, he ran into stark tragedy. Widespread and prolonged illness among the Negroes had caused the death of some of the most valuable of them. Johnny did not describe the nature of their illness, but his correspondence suggests that it must have reached epidemic proportions. Even so, on September 12 he sent, as prearranged, a number of his Negroes to David Crenshaw Barrow's salt works in Florida. As if the illness of Cobb's Negroes was not enough, his swine became infested with cholera. September was unseasonably hot, dry, and dusty. During this month alone 135 hogs died on the Sumter place. Fortunately most of the fatalities occurred among the sows and small shoats, not the fattening hogs.[14]

Despite the discouraging prospects for his next year's meat supply, Johnny had to trade this important product of the plantation for other necessities. In September he exchanged it pound for pound for sugar, acquiring a hogshead of the latter from the government, "It was like the Thompson door knocker," he boasted, ". . . cheap and I bought it."[15] He planned to ship it to his mother in Athens within a week or ten days. Minor needs of the family also received Johnny's attention. Miss Sawyer's request for calico did not go unheeded. Since the brown serge Lucy wanted could not be found, her resourceful husband recommended that she buy some green and "swap" it for brown. Lucy's craving for material with which to make veils was gratified. Nor did the young bride's feet escape the attention of her provident spouse. She must send her size to Howell, Jr., in Atlanta, so he could have a pair of shoes made to order.[16]

Although the Cobb plantations had always been primarily given to cotton growing, yet in the days of John B. Lamar much food had been produced on them. They were therefore not put to producing something totally new when John Cobb took them over late in 1862. That they were well stocked with bacon, lard, and corn a year later is not surprising. Unfortunately the Confederate purchasing agent, whose duty it was to procure as much food as he could, often lacked facilities for moving and storing the bulkier products such as corn. As the agent accumulated these products, he often found himself at the mercy of the planter for storage space. Late in September of 1863 the purchasing agent in southwest Georgia reported that 300,000 corn sacks had been sent to Charleston to be exchanged for sand bags. Until he received some corn sacks, he informed Johnny that the corn purchased months before at the Cobb plantation in Sumter County could not be moved. Also short of hands, the agent tried to hire refugees from Mississippi.[17] How this turned out, he failed to record.

Annoying as the problem of storage was, Confederate authorities actually made it worse. They ordered Cobb to pay a tax of $2,000 on government corn stored on his Sumter place. He naturally refused to pay it, charging that Confederate tax policy was an outrage. To Lucy he wrote: "The last Congress were the biggest fools in the world, except the men . . . appointed to carry out the laws . . . and I don't think this world or any other are ahead of them for want of sense."[18] After weeks of delay during which time Johnny made a trip to Forsyth to confer with a tax official, the government decided the Cobbs would not have to pay the tax on Confederate corn stored in their Sumter cribs.[19] Thus ended an awkward situation for John Cobb and the Confederacy.

Johnny did not spend all his time arguing with tax officers, swapping meat for sugar, and searching for calico and material with which to make veils. Macon was at this time a bustling center. To this middle Georgia city came countless civilians and soldiers. Some lingered, others went on. Among the soldiers who came to Macon in early September 1863 was a Major McLaws en route from Virginia to Florida. To Johnny he related a story that reveals something of the character of the Rebel soldier. The major had taken part in the Battle of Fredericksburg. No member of the Cobb family could ever forget this engagement, for it was there, in fact in the garden of his maternal ancestors, that Thomas R. R. Cobb was killed on December 13, 1862. Cobb had fallen near a stone wall where the fighting had been fierce. During the action a chicken flew to the top of the wall and remained there until the battle ended. Afterwards the fowl was captured and it became the possession of the army. McLaws was taking it to Florida for delivery to Colonel Delaney, then commanding Cobb's old outfit.[20] Like the Yankee soldier and the "doughboy" and the "G. I." of the twentieth century, Johnny Reb had his idiosyncrasies.

While Lucy Barrow Cobb could not immediately be with her busy husband in Macon, she was fortunate in another respect. The Cobbs at once accepted her as one of the family. Without a mother of her own since she was ten, the young bride was pleased to be permitted to address Mary Ann as "Mama."[21] To the four younger Cobb children she was "Sister Lucy." In September 1863, when Mary Ann joined "the Genl." in Atlanta, Lucy took over the Cobb household.[22] She made at least one report of her stewardship to the elder Mrs. Cobb. Except for Andrew, the lone boy, she wrote that the youngsters were well. His slight cold was caused by what Lucy strangely referred to as "the change from Summer to Winter." The mother's order to put flannels on the children produced a minor crisis when the key to the box which contained them could not be found. However, Lucy assured the elder Mrs. Cobb that there was no cause for alarm, as the children were not entirely unprotected. Lizzie had been wearing a flannel shirt for over a week, Sarah was making use of Andrew's flannel jackets, and Mary Ann, the oldest daughter, discovered that hers had not been locked up. But, wrote the tactful Lucy a few days before she expected Mrs. Cobb to return, "we really begin to need you."[23]

Mary Ann Cobb's visit to Atlanta in September of 1863 had been her first opportunity to observe "the Genl." at work. At this time he was preparing to defend Atlanta and trying to supply men and ordnance for General Bragg's army, then engaged in the crucial Chattanooga Campaign.[24] Both she and her husband were disturbed by Bragg's ineffectiveness and by the President's refusal to replace him with General Joseph E. Johnston.[25] On her return to Athens later in the month Mary Ann redoubled her efforts in behalf of the cause. Unfortunately all Athenians did not share her enthusiasm. That both she and Lucy's father should have difficulty in arousing interest in receiving and caring for wounded and sick soldiers grieved her. Particularly upsetting was the insolence of many women of Athens. Said one whose help she solicited: "The whole Southern Confederacy was not worth a thimble full of her blood."[26] Many wondered why the army, which they accused of already stripping north Georgia, could not look after its own sick and wounded. When a regiment of cavalry on its way to north Georgia stopped in Athens a few days, Mary Ann reported that many townspeople wished the horsemen would leave as their presence was making it difficult to get "butter-eggs-beef or anything." Mary Ann was satisfied such people would "welcome the Yankee General," for they believed that to win forgiveness one simply declared he had always opposed secession. "Deluded fools" was her way of referring to them, bitterly observing they would do well to get back to the "wash tub and cook pot" as the servants of their former employees. She predicted, however, that many would require their "fat arms and legs" bound in Yankee irons before they were convinced "secession was right."[27]

Home in early October for the second time since his wedding, Johnny too was upset over the behavior of many Athenians. Hotel owners were gouging refugees with high prices, serving bad food, and offering poor accommodations. Too many were busy making money; too few were engaged in patriotic endeavors. In young Cobb's opinion Athens was able to care for as many as 2,000 sick and wounded by making use of university buildings and the town hall. Should this be done, Athens would then compare favorably with such Georgia towns as Eatonton and Milledgeville. While Johnny and his mother agreed that many local townsfolk were generous and sympathetic, Mary Ann probably summed up the feelings of both when she wrote that some Athenians were " . . . cold as toads and as close as Lucifer."[28]

It was at this time that the Cobbs made preliminary arrangements for the family's annual visit to Macon. They would leave Athens early in November. Lucy would, of course, go to Macon; on this all were agreed, but whether she would accompany Mary Ann and the children remained to be decided. Mary Ann's plan to take along her oldest daughter's French teacher met with an objection from Johnny. Because the teacher was a foreigner, she might "inculcate his sister with foreign notions." Disgusted with her son's attitude, Mrs. Cobb was determined to take the French teacher to Macon. For the smaller children "the Genl." had bought two ponies. They were to bear the reverent names of "Hallelujah" and "Amen" respectively and were to be in Macon when the Cobbs arrived.[29]

On Saturday, October 9, Johnny left for Macon via Atlanta and Forsyth. In Atlanta he joined his brother Howell, Jr. They spent the night with their Aunt Laura, wife of Colonel Luther Glenn. Instead of attending church with his father on Sunday, Johnny went with his brother to visit friends at a nearby military camp. This turned out to be a happy choice, for he learned afterwards that Judge A. B. Longstreet had preached and "his sermon was so long that even his friends rejoiced when he concluded."[30]

Atlanta was an exciting place during the fall of 1863. Men and supplies were choking its streets and all roads leading into it. Attention was fixed in the direction of the Tennessee line. Just across it was Bragg's army. Could it save Georgia from the Yankees? Many doubted Bragg's capabilities. Even the President may have had misgivings. At any rate, he was in Atlanta conferring with Howell Cobb about the time Johnny reached the city. On October 9 Davis left for a visit with his favorite general, the elder Cobb, whose feeling for Bragg was well known, escorting him only part of the way.[31]

Howell may already have concluded that much of north Georgia was to be overrun. Whatever his opinion, he did tell Johnny that he would soon move the Georgia State Guard's headquarters to Macon, approximately one hundred miles south of Atlanta. Pleased with such a prospect, young Cobb wrote his wife on October 10 that "it will suit *our* family much better."

As John Cobb resumed the lonely trip back to the Bear's Den on October 12, he could look forward with reasonable assurance that within a month Lucy would join him in Macon. Moreover, the transfer of his father's headquarters to that city was now a possibility. For the remainder of October and for the first days of November Johnny planned and carried out an extensive itinerary. It took him to Sumter County, thence to Florida, back to Atlanta via Albany and Macon, then to Columbus and Milledgeville, and finally home to Macon on November 4. Most of his travelling was done by train, though in Florida he sometimes went by steamboat. While in that state he visited Lucy's father and her brother James, reporting the latter had fallen in love with one of Quincy's comely widows.[32]

Johnny had gone to Florida in search of a lost shipment of shoes which his Negroes needed badly, and to bring to Macon for his own convenience the buggy and horses used by his father while he was in Quincy.[33] Exhausted by his travels, young Cobb wrote Lucy from the Bear's Den on the last of October that, though "[I'm] in my house . . . it does not feel so, for you are not here." She must get his mother off to Macon at once, and what was vastly more important to him the younger Mrs. Cobb must come along, for pleaded Johnny, ". . . in these troubled times there is no telling what may turn up any day that may separate us for some time." This was particularly so, continued Johnny, with a person like himself, "who is in some doubt whether he is liable to conscription or not." Some day when he least expected he feared an officer "may take it into his head to decide the question for me." For good measure the lonely young man added yet another inducement to bring Lucy to Macon. The house, he boasted, had been thoroughly cleaned, carpets had been put down, and the master of the Bear's Den was prepared to "wind up" one year of "housekeep."

If Lucy had any doubts about going to Macon immediately, Johnny's exhortations of October 31 ended them. On November 4 she wrote her husband that she would arrive on the eleventh. Overjoyed at this news, he wrote on the sixth: "Four more days my darling and you will be here." These would, he added, be long days to him. Already he had sent a wagon to the Sumter place for geese, ducks, chickens, and eggs to feed the crowd that was soon to arrive at the Bear's Den. When he left for Sumter a few days later, it was his plan to return in time to meet Lucy at the depot. She was to come via Augusta and presumably to be escorted by Johnny's brother Lamar. Mary Ann Cobb thought it an outrage that Johnny should permit Lucy to take her first trip without him as escort. Only a woman of sense would not be offended, she wrote her son, who in turn assured Lucy that he knew he had such a wife and was not afraid to take the risk. And so Johnny probably was at the depot to meet his wife's train at 5:25 A.M. on November 11. At any rate, so he had planned.[34]

Whether all went according to John Cobb's schedule is not known. However, Lucy did reach Macon, for on November 16 she wrote her father that Mary Ann Cobb, the four Cobb children, Lamar and his wife, she and Johnny, and some others had all been converted into one large French family under the direction of the French teacher Mary Ann had brought along. In a month, boasted Lucy, "we will be able to *parley-vous* with any Frenchman." Lucy also reported that she had been riding a kicking pony and the result was that her hand trembled so greatly that she could hardly write.

To this Johnny inserted an objection, ascribing the state of her hand to a cold room. She had been too lazy, he charged, to have a fire made. "I have had one made," he continued, "and she will be warm during the balance of the letter."[35] At last Johnny and Lucy were together as permanently as the times would permit.

CHAPTER VII

War Takes Another Dear One

LUCY BARROW COBB was to spend three happy months in Macon, sharing wartime comforts and miseries with the Cobbs and their numerous guests. Cobbs and Barrows seem to have made the Bear's Den their most important place of call during the winter of 1863-64. There were dinners, weddings, and parties and there were trips to Milledgeville, Athens, Atlanta, and Quincy. Occasionally Lucy would go with her husband to the plantations. When he went to the "Hurricane," the Cobb plantation in Baldwin County, she sometimes went with him as far as Milledgeville, the state capital. There she would spend time visiting relatives and friends, while Johnny transacted his business at the plantation.[1] Often he went alone, humorously protesting as he was once leaving for Sumter County that his mother had "pushed him off."[2]

It was not all fun and frolic for Lucy at the Bear's Den. She had her share of colds, Grandma Pope warning that "frolicing always ends in sickness."[3] The young bride's health had become a source of worry to both her father and grandmother. She assured them, however, that her "cold and cough" were not serious and that, except for chapped lips, she had full possession of her "health and spirits."[4] In mid-winter Lucy shivered with the others when the firewood gave out and the mud was so deep the supply wagon broke down on its way from the "Hurricane."[5]

Wood was not the only article in short supply at the Bear's Den during the winter of 1863-64. Nor was the Bear's Den the only quarter to register a Cobb plea for help. From Atlanta, where "the Genl." had been eating beef until he was about to "begin to bellow," came a demand for relief. Cobb wanted pork, both sausages and backbone.[6] He got his pork, but down in middle Georgia sausage making was becoming increasingly difficult because of the scarcity of both red and black pepper. Moreover, the corn crop at the "Hurricane," the plantation upon which the Cobbs now depended for supplies, had fallen far below Johnny's expectations.[7] There were other troubles too. David Crenshaw Barrow's salt business in Florida was not going well. Now helping his father-in-law in this enterprise, young Cobb was finding it beset with major difficulties. Shipping costs were heavy for one thing, and besides there were such perils as shrinkage, stealing, and seizures. Yet to abandon the undertaking was believed inadvisable, for at least it had the merit of providing salt for the Cobbs and Barrows.[8]

Although the Cobbs and Barrows lived less elegantly than was their habit before the war, yet compared to the meager comforts of many people they continued to fare well during the winter of 1863-64. Food was ample and the Bear's Den was not long without wood. Johnny could return from town in midwinter, eat a hearty meal, then comfortably seat himself before the fireplace, which consumed wood at the rate of one dollar per hour, and while warming his feet and smoking his cigar alternately gaze at the fire and a well-filled box of wood. Indeed, the Cobbs, having recently acquired a fifth plantation, were now among the wealthiest people in Georgia. Against this "rich planter class" there was a growing resentment. Mary Ann Cobb was aware of this, once complaining to her husband that there was more equality in the privations and hardships borne by the rich and poor than the latter "dream of."[9] With incredible naivete, she convinced herself of the validity of her claim by adding, "for with five plantations we are restricted to the use of the proceeds from only the poorest."[10]

That Howell Cobb was a generous man few would deny. Happy over his recent promotion to major general and proud of the Confederacy, he would give a demonstration of a planter's liberality.[11] Thus early in 1864 he journeyed to Americus, Sumter County, to address the people of southwest Georgia on the state of the country. In the course of what he was to describe to President Davis as "the right

kind of speech," Cobb boasted that no soldier's wife had ever
left his "den empty handed."[12] A few days later two elderly
wives decided to test the General's claim. They hired a horse
and wagon and headed for the plantation he had recently
purchased in Newton County. Upon meeting Johnny, they
informed him they had come to get something to eat. He
refused them syrup, sold them one hundred pounds of bacon
for $24, this being all the money they had, and then proceeded
to tell them nothing more could be purchased at the plantation.[13]

The next day Johnny delivered 1,000 pounds of bacon
to the Inferior Court, "and in that way," he wrote his father,
"I hope to be clear of trouble in the future." In conclusion,
he warned that it did not "pay to make too strong a speech
in the county where your own plantations are."[14] From Mary
Ann came another warning: "Be a little more cautious hereafter in what you say on this subject." The rich, she explained,
must not expect to be rewarded during the war, but by doing their duty for God and country they were assured of the
Almighty's blessing. By comparison with this assurance the
praise of man, inspired by the generous behavior of the rich,
"is as evanescent as his breath is perishing."[15]

Although there was really no threat of a food shortage
at the Bear's Den during the winter of 1863-64, Mary Ann
Cobb was nevertheless worried about the problem of providing for her big family. She was certain the problem would
grow more rather than less vexing. On January 11 she wrote
her husband that if he were soon to be located in Macon "it
will be so cozy to draw wood from the Quarter Master's Department." A few days later she asked Johnny if he could
possibly arrange with the commissary to assure enough corn
to feed the stock.[16]

Despite Johnny's good production record in 1863, he
shared his mother's uneasiness.[17] The reason was simple
enough: the Rebel army in north Georgia was not doing well.
In November Bragg had fallen back to Ringgold. Howell
thought this "the greatest defeat of the war."[18] Disaster "was
upon us," he lamented.[19] It was at this time that he called for
pork to bolster his sagging spirits, and then hastened to Richmond again to urge the President to replace Bragg. The

Georgian hoped Lee would be sent south; but Joseph E. Johnston was to come instead.[20] Mary Ann responded to Confederate reverses by asserting that God was on the Rebel side, "or else Gen. Bragg's feeble army would have been driven before the enemy like chaff before the wind."[21] Johnny ascribed part of the Confederacy's afflictions to Jews and Yankee speculators.[22] His father was kinder to the Jews, publicly charging in mid-January at Macon that in "the business of extortion there are many *uncircumcised* Jews."[23]

Lucy was a real comfort to the Cobbs during the last days of 1863. Her "loving and gentle heart" and her wholesome sense of humor were antidotes for the strains created by almost three years of war. When she was not attending a party with Johnny or accompanying him to one of the plantations, she was studying French, entertaining the Cobb children, or writing a letter to the folks in Athens.[24] Her sister Clara and "the Genl." spent the Christmas holidays at the Bear's Den. It was a particularly happy occasion for Lucy and the elder Cobb. Both were deeply moved by the "little ones gathered around" Mary Ann's knee, unaware of the world beyond the fireside and contented with their apples, oranges, popcorn balls, crackers, candy, and books.[25]

Amidst the jollities of the holiday season Johnny was making plans to take Lucy to Florida. Mrs. William E. Kilcrease, the Quincy widow engaged to Lucy's brother James, had extended the young couple an invitation to visit her. Johnny expected to combine business with pleasure by calling at the elder Barrow's salt works on Florida's Gulf coast. Late in December 1863 tentative plans called for the couple's departure some time during the latter part of January 1864. At length, all arrangements for a two-weeks trip to begin on February 5 were completed.[26]

Whether Lucy and Johnny actually made the Florida visit they planned is uncertain. Should they have done so, it is unlikely they saw James. Now a lieutenant colonel in the Sixty-fourth Georgia Volunteers, young Barrow and his unit had been ordered to Savannah early in the year and then almost immediately called back to Florida.[27] By mid-February General Beauregard in Charleston had succeeded in concentrating over 5,000 Rebel troops around Lake City in north central Florida. It may be assumed that James was there and not at Quincy, approximately one hundred miles due west, at the time his sister and Johnny were to have arrived in the latter city. Meanwhile, approximately an equal number of Federal troops had landed at Jacksonville and promptly had begun moving westward. On February 20, which was about the time Johnny had planned to be back in Macon, the two armies clashed in the area of Lake City. During the battle James Barrow was shot through the heart and died immediately.[28]

In Macon Johnny received a dispatch from Tom Barrow on February 23 announcing the death of James. The body would reach Macon the next day. Immediately informing David Crenshaw Barrow in Athens of his son's death, Johnny wrote that he and Lucy would accompany the body.[29] Late on February 24 the young couple reached Athens with the remains. The next day James was buried in Oconee Cemetery. Later that same day Johnny wrote his father of the elder Barrow's wish that Howell Cobb write James' obituary. Howell responded with a moving tribute.[30] He had known James well "in the family circle, around the campfire, in the battle-field, in the various duties and relations of life." Admitting to a friendship that was "almost paternal," Cobb did not spare the superlatives as he acclaimed the virtues of James Barrow than whom none was more deserving of his country's gratitude.

Because James was the recognized favorite of the family, the Barrows were deeply distressed.[31] Lucy especially was touched. For several days after the funeral she tried on numerous occasions to write her brother Tom a letter of "sympathy and consolation as only a fellow sufferer could." Each time, however, blinding tears would fall and choking, convulsive sobs would rise to halt the effort. Her kindest thoughts and sympathies, as well as those of all the Barrows, were with Tom, alone in Florida during the family's ordeal in Athens.[32]

Finally, on March 1, with Johnny back in Macon, Lucy wrote Tom from Athens.[33] How proud of the "noble" James she had been, and to think of him gone forever brought such a "sense of desolation and wretchedness" that she sometimes felt she would be glad to die and be with him. Yet she mourned not for him as she would for one without hope. His had been a righteous life, his death that of a righteous man. How comforting the thought! Her tears ceased to flow and she could "almost rejoice" that a merciful God had taken her dear brother from "this world of care and trial." How tranquilizing the trust of the harassed Job: "Great things doeth He that we cannot comprehend," but "what we know not now we shall know hereafter." This, explained Lucy, was the only way to think of their dear brother's death. No "bitter, revengeful vow" against "his murderers" must pass Tom's lips or even enter his mind. This must be left in the hands of a "wise and just God." At "His hands" James' "murderers *will* have their reward." Indeed, Lucy seemed to envy James. Three days after her touching letter to Tom she wrote Johnny: "Oh! What would I not give to die as he has died!" Thereupon she concluded her reference to James with the apocalyptic observation that perhaps before the end of the year "we all shall envy him his happiness."[34]

For months the sad memories of James slept lightly on the edge of Lucy's consciousness. The wind and rain of March often quickened them. She was unable to sleep, she wrote her husband at this time, "for thinking of the lone sleeper out in the graveyard." Seated around warm, cheerful fireplaces before bed time, "*we*," she sadly observed, were in "full life and vigor—and *he* so lately the strongest—bravest of all—lying low and lifeless with the rough wind and rain beating mercilessly upon him." She could almost see "his pale—still—face—and rigid limbs lying right before me and all exposed to the fury of the storm."[35]

Mrs. Kilcrease, James' betrothed, also helped to revive the sad memories. She had not attended the funeral, but three weeks afterwards wrote the Barrows a letter which Lucy described as full of "sorrow and sympathy." Lucy wished to write her, but they were not "formally acquainted." Hence if Johnny and Lucy did make their planned trip to Florida, they did not see Mrs. Kilcrease. So Lucy sought Johnny's advice. Without waiting for it, however, she wrote Mrs. Kilcrease in mid-March, hoping to give "a bit of comfort to that mourning heart."[36]

Chapter VIII

War Comes Closer

Early March 1864 opened another chapter in the lives of Mr. and Mrs. John A. Cobb. The exquisite joy of the three months they had lately spent together at the Bear's Den was eclipsed by James Barrow's death. Within a week after his funeral they were again separated, Lucy remaining in Athens and Johnny returning to Macon. Lucy soon adjusted to the loss of her brother. Although she frequently went to the cemetery with her grandmother, the young bride was to find many other things to occupy her time and talents. In the cozy Barrow sitting room she would often write Johnny, her attention sometimes divided between him, a stick of molasses candy, a bolt of homewoven flannel, and a lively conversation. At other times she would join the needle-work experts, Miss Sawyer and Grandma Pope, or she might amuse herself by observing her younger brothers delving into the mysteries of long division and cube root. She also read, perhaps *Les Miserables*, a copy of which Johnny sent her soon after he returned to Macon.[1] The Barrow household was a lively place. Often it was crowded, at times Lucy having to share her bed with two others. One morning she arose and described her condition as "half cooked" because both the quarters and the atmosphere had been so "close." Nevertheless Lucy seemed to thrive, Grandma Pope assuring her in mid-March that she was looking "fatter and rosier" than when she had come home in February.[2]

In Macon Johnny was going about matters with his customary "Cobb-like gravity." There were the dull trips to the plantations and then back to the Bear's Den which, despite the presence of many Cobbs, offered him cold comfort now that his wife was absent. He was not feeling well at this time and his letters reveal a marked dullness. His major interest continued to be his lovely wife. That she could not be constantly at his side naturally distressed him, and may have been the reason for his increasing concern with trivia and his growing mood of haughtiness.[3] At times he could even be arrogant to Lucy, herself a model of perspicacity, understanding, humility, and tender affection. In one of his surlier moments, Johnny rebuked her for failing to sign and address "on the inside" a letter in which she expressed her tenderest feelings for her dead brother and prophesied that perhaps all would envy him before the year's end.[4] "If it was not for the envelope," complained Johnny, "no one would know who it was for or who from."[5] Several days before the rebuke arrived, but too late to head it off, Lucy had already explained her lapse. The letter was to have been signed "Cassandra," but a little research disclosed that Cassandra's prophesies never came true. She then thought of "Norn" as perhaps a more appropriate prophetess, but, still undecided, she did not attach that name either. The letter was put aside, Lucy became busy with other things, and at the last moment it was hastily sealed unsigned. She apologized for writing about something of which she knew so little, and reminded her husband that she had "a due share of foibles" and that he must bear with her patiently inasmuch as "I have the same trials of patience from you."[6]

Then came Johnny's rebuke. To it Lucy responded with vigor and dispatch.[7] For his gratification she would "in future have a proper and becoming address at the beginning of my letters and a respectful signature at the close." As evidence of her intent she greeted him with a formal: "Capt. John A. Cobb, My dear sir:"; and ornately closed with: "I am very respectfully yours, Lucy Barrow Cobb." Uncertain of the precise form her spouse wished, she sarcastically noted that she would be "exceedingly obliged . . . if in your next you would communicate your exact views upon the question—as to style—phraseology, etc." In digust she added: "But let us have done with this nonsense." If the pompous Johnny had not yet been discomposed, the blistering that followed must surely have made him so. Vexed by his petty remarks about her earlier slips, Lucy sternly warned that if he thought her response a show of "perverseness beyond endurance . . . we are at 'Quits.' " With the agility of a panther, the wounded spouse seized the offensive, charging her husband with a breach of etiquette in the very letter containing his reprimand. He was anxious that his wife return to Macon, but neither he nor her brother Pope was free to escort her. Exultantly she asked, "and you would not have me put myself in the hands of the conductor, would you?" Whatever the degree of Lucy's anger, it soon passed. Even her response to Johnny's rebuke carried an invitation that he treat the affair as a minor aberration. Thus she expressed concern over his health and assured him that her heart was full of love "for the best old Bluebeard in the world." Her letters were soon to lose their rigid formality and Johnny became "my gude mon." So ended a lovers' epistolary spat.

The John A. Cobbs were to have other differences, some of them more fundamental than their altercation over how to open and close a love letter. For example, they held sharply contrasting views on the nature of the Negro. While one finds few references to the Negro in their letters of the Civil War years, yet the subject does not go unmentioned. Shortly after returning to Macon in March 1864, Johnny reported that a slave named Anderson Iverson had driven "Old Mars," a favorite horse of Mary Ann Cobb, from Macon to the Baldwin plantation. Upon arrival the horse dropped dead, because, charged young Cobb, he had been driven too hard. Mary Ann ordered that Anderson be banished "from her presence forever . . . kept at hard labor under Mr. J. D. Collins [the overseer] for a term of years." Her son hoped this order would never be revoked.[8] Like many of his contemporaries, Johnny believed the "negro affiliates with the monkey race, and consequently has no soul to save." Lucy rejected this notion and argued with her husband over it, once chiding him with having an "easy-going, quiet conscience" and never thinking of burdening his soul with the "salvation of a negro."[9]

Lucy and Johnny would seem to have had a normal share of differences. In the written exchanges over them Lucy appears generally as the more deft. Perhaps it was her stinging inquiry whether a train conductor's duties included escorting a young married woman that stirred Johnny to action. At any rate, soon afterwards he went to Athens to escort his wife to Macon.[10] Lucy's visit to the "Vatican," as she now referred to the Bear's Den, was a short one. By mid-April she was back in Athens, Johnny confessing at this time that after changing his mind almost daily, he had finally decided "it is best for you to remain with me no matter where that is."[11] He was anxious to make a "housekeeper" of his wife and at last the prospect looked encouraging. His father, confided Johnny, was preparing to buy a house in Americus. The furniture in Athens was to be moved there, so that in case Macon became unsafe the Cobbs would have a place to go. Southwest Georgia was to become the safest place in the state, continued Johnny, once the plan to relocate the prisoners at Andersonville was carried out.

Major General Howell Cobb made his decision to buy a house in Americus soon after he arrived in Macon in early April to set up headquarters for a newly authorized state home guard. With the expiration in February 1864 of the Georgia Guard, which Cobb had administered from Atlanta since its formation the previous fall, the Confederate Congress, largely in response to his importunities, empowered him to create a "minute man" corps, to be known as the Georgia Reserve Force. It was to be composed of all ablebodied men between the ages of 17-18, 45-50, and those persons on detail from the Provisional Army. For use only in local emergencies, Reserve personnel would otherwise be engaged in such civilian duties as contributed to the war effort.[12]

The nature of this new command was a foretoken of the rough days that lay ahead. About one month after Cobb had set up headquarters in Macon General Sherman started a drive that by early September was to carry him all the way to Atlanta. Cobb was anxious for a first-hand view of the situation confronting Johnston's Army of Tennessee. In June he therefore paid Johnston a visit. He saw how desperate the situation was and could hardly have been surprised on learning in mid-July that Sherman was already south of the Chattahoochee River, within less than ten miles of Atlanta. Nor is it likely that he was surprised a few days later to learn also that his good friend Johnston had been replaced by General John B. Hood. Cobb thought "Old Joe" Johnston far too valuable to be set adrift; so he invited him to Macon. There the former commander of the Army of Tennessee helped with the organization of the Georgia Reserve Force, remaining long enough to participate in the Battle of East Macon on July 30.[13]

Meanwhile John A. Cobb was making preparations to move cattle, mules, and young Negro men from the Baldwin place to the plantations in the Americus area, now felt to be about the only part of Georgia safe from the threat of Yankee raiding parties. What could not be readily moved to southwestern Georgia was brought to Macon, in the belief that raiders would be less likely to molest this area than that of the state capital around Milledgeville. While Johnny was in southwest Georgia during the latter part of April, Lucy, escorted by her brother Pope, who was now on the elder Cobb's staff in Macon, made the trip from Athens to her uncle William McKinley's plantation near Milledgeville. There she ate fish from the river, strolled over the rolling hills, and observed regular hours of sleep and rest. So beneficial was her visit that she boasted to Mary Ann Cobb about how wonderfully her cheeks were filling out and predicted Johnny would have reason to be proud of her when she reached the Bear's Den a few days later.[14]

Early in May, Lucy was again at the Bear's Den. Much had happened since her visit of less than a month before. Her father-in-law was now well along with the work of organizing the Georgia Reserve Force. On his staff was her brother Pope. As there was no chance for promotion, Pope was considering a transfer to other duty. Because Lucy believed he was able to correct her faults without either ceremony or fear of hurting her pride, she wished him to remain in Macon. She had recently come to feel that Johnny was deliberately avoiding the role of helpful critic. Although she did not mention it, perhaps her husband remembered too well the late encounter with his redoubtable spouse.[15]

It has been observed that the prison at Andersonville became a subject of more than passing interest to the Cobbs once "the Genl." decided to buy a house for his family in nearby Americus. On order from Richmond, Howell made an inspection of the prison early in May. Lucy wrote her father that the elder Cobb "rode all over the camp," that he "says it is not such a horrible, loathsome place, as it has been represented," and that "indeed [he] seems to think they [the prisoners] are as well treated as they deserve to be."[16] The growing bitterness of Georgians toward the "invader," now bearing down on Atlanta, was reflected in the treatment of the prisoners at Andersonville as well as in the general attitude toward those who were so unfortunate as to be captured. About two weeks after Lucy reported on Howell Cobb's visit to Andersonville Pope wrote her: "That infamous wretch Genl. [Truman] Seymour . . . arrived yesterday."[17] Captured at Spotsylvania and sent to Macon for detention, Seymour had been the Federal commander during the Florida campaign in which their brother James was killed.[18]

A house in Americus was a part of the Cobb plan to survive. Even though it was to be a third home, this did not seem unreasonable to the Cobbs or the Barrows. Both had been affluent before the war, and they were now simply acting as they had always acted. When confronted with survival they exhibited a galaxy of emotions and reactions. Often a single act can be at once pathetic and amusing. An example was the fate of a box the Barrows sent in the spring of 1864 to Lucy and Pope, both then in Macon. It was filled with rare fabrics and precious whiskey. From the fabrics Lucy herself was to make much-needed dresses, while the whiskey was for Pope. En route one of the bottles of whiskey was broken, the dry goods soaking up what was to have dampened palates and induced conviviality among the Confederate officer and his friends. One can imagine Lucy's relief when examination disclosed the whiskey-soaked fabrics had not been injured. It is no less difficult to picture the dejection at the Bear's Den when it was learned, as Lucy so tersely put it, that "the whiskey is all gone."[19]

It was at this time that Lucy came under the spell of "some invisible hand" which "seems drawing me to . . . Bro. Tom . . . and Mrs. Kilcrease."[20] Accordingly, she made preparations for her and Johnny to join the elder Barrow's small party as in mid-May it was to pass through Macon on the way to Florida. By early June Johnny was already back in Macon and his wife on her way to the Barrow salt works at St. Marks.[21] Lest her husband be unduly alarmed, Lucy assured him there was no danger from the enemy. "Why my 'Gude Mon,' " she quipped, "instead of running the risk of putting an end to my life, I am going towards the 'Fountain of life!' " From Newport's Sulphur Springs, the fountain of perpetual youth which the Spaniard had vainly sought and whose waters "the Genl." believed "a panacea to every ill," she would drink and "receive renewed life and vigor, and return . . . a changed creature in more respects than one."[22]

Lucy's Florida travels took her to Quincy, St. Marks, Newport, and Tallahassee. In Quincy social demands were burdensome; she and her companions sought various means of escape, including the rendition of excuses with such "bombastic elegance" that the poor hostesses thought they had "blundered terribly in asking ladies whose time was so fully occupied." Cousin Bessie became proficient in the fabrication and delivery of such fables. When her talents seemed too feeble, the whole party would pray for rain that they might have an excuse to sit in the carriage and "send in our card, with regrets that the rain" prevented a personal call. Although her father lectured Lucy about the sinfulness of such prayers, her poetic response was completely to the point. If he knew "how from my very soul I loathe this heartless, senseless business, of making and receiving fashionable visits, uttering the same silly nothings at each place, and receiving the same simpering compliments and acquiescences—he would think it a subject for earnest prayer to be rid of them now and *evermore*."[23]

Johnny had good reason to worry about his wife's safety. With only small detachments of cavalry defending Florida's extensive coast line, the state was literally unprotected. After consulting with "the Genl." early in June, young Cobb advised his father-in-law to put aside for family needs a two years' supply of salt and then get out of Florida once and for all by selling the vulnerable salt works there.[24]

To both Lucy and Johnny the events through which they lived during mid-summer 1864 must have seemed in retrospect a fitting prelude to the disaster Georgia experienced during the last four months of that year. As Sherman's army moved steadily toward Atlanta in the summer, the fruitless resistance of the Army of Tennessee spread infection throughout the state. A contagion of despondency was borne on the wings of fact and rumor. Whether fact or rumor, the story about the wife and son of the late John H. Lumpkin was especially shocking to the Cobbs. Lumpkin had been a United States congressman from Georgia's old Fifth District. He and Johnny's father had been the closest of friends. On June 5 Johnny wrote his wife that Mrs. Lumpkin had received the thanks of an Ohio captain for furnishing him and his company "fine wine and other delicacies." More distressing was the story that Lumpkin's son, formerly a lieutenant in the Confederate service, had deserted "to the enemy." Before the war the Lumpkins had lived in Rome, Georgia. From Athens, the state's other city named for the classical lands, came signs of apathy and fright. From it, where he had gone in mid-June to inspect the "Mitchell Thunderbolts," Pope Barrow reported the officers of this unit of the Georgia Reserve Force were engaged in petty and malicious squabbles, that none really wished to fight, and that he could find only two "Thunderbolts" ready for inspection.[25] On July 11 Mary Ann Cobb, also writing from Athens, expressed the fear that her friends and neighbors would succumb to the "terrible panic" which was rumored to have overtaken Atlantans.[26]

That persistent foe of the Cobbs, Governor Joe Brown, decided he would have a hand in saving Atlanta. In June he stormed into the city with his "Pets," the officers of a nondescript unit known as "Joe Brown's Malish." Upon reaching Atlanta the wily governor boasted that he would personally lead his "Pets" into battle "when the time comes." Johnny hoped the time would "soon come and that his [Brown's] time may come at the same time." Young Cobb sincerely believed the governor's death would be "a blessing to the country."[27] But Brown was not to die; he was to become an even more implacable foe of the Cobbs instead.

To meet the emergency that faced Georgia in the summer of 1864 all males between the ages of 16 and 60 had become liable for military service with either the Confederate Provisional Army, the Georgia Reserve Force, or "Joe Brown's

Malish." Under these circumstances planters were hard put. Johnny was able to save but two of his overseers. One declared he was too sick to go to camp, and this, observed Johnny, "makes his case all right," for he was also "too smart to get well before this *emergency* is over." Johnny was able to hold a second overseer by arranging a contract with the Confederate government to fatten 200 mules. To this assignment he had one of his Sumter County overseers detailed. Thus with two overseers, instead of the five he once had, Johnny tried to keep the Cobb plantations running.[28]

Meanwhile Lucy, Bly, and Cousin Bessie left Florida for William McKinley's plantation near Milledgeville. En route they stopped over in Macon and Lucy must surely have intended returning to be with her husband on their first wedding anniversary on July 29. On the eve of their anniversary Johnny wrote Lucy that he hoped the second year of their marriage would bring peace and quiet to their country, so "that we can enjoy each other's society more." Peace must have seemed an eternity away as both Johnny and his wife busily searched for security in the midst of the bad news from Atlanta and the rumors of raids that were headed toward the state capital. Fearing such a raid, Johnny advised Lucy late in July that in case one was known to be on its way to Milledgeville she should try to reach Macon by train. Failing in this her Uncle William was "to put you all in carriages, buggies, wagons, etc. and send you off down towards Washington County and let you hide out until it passes."[29]

On her wedding anniversary Lucy was in bed with hot bricks, sipping tansy tea between doses of Jacob's Cordial. Her head ached, her heart ached, every bone in her body ached, all rendered endurable, she wrote Johnny on this day, "only by the thought that you knew nothing of my suffering." For two weary days she lay in bed at her uncle's plantation, thinking of the year that was ending. What "a bit of time" it seemed to her, yet the events of ages had been squeezed into it. "What might not be said of it! its loves, its joys, its hopes, and fears—its bitter, bitter griefs, and the sweet lessons of resignation and trust in God which have now and then come to gladden our hearts!" Late in the afternoon of "our wedding day" Lucy dressed, drank a glass of blackberry wine, and managed to "drag her trembling limbs" to the steps of the front portico, her favorite resort at this hour of the day.[30]

Thus ensconced, Lucy divided her attention between writing to Johnny and watching a gorgeous sunset. Suddenly she beheld the little runners from town "tearing 'round the circle like mad." She believed they must have some exciting news. And so they had: 6,000 Yankees were at Monticello, about thirty miles to the northwest. Scouts reported that they were to be formed into two parties, one to strike in the direction of Macon and the other to move toward Milledgeville. Precipitantly the household collected on the steps "to wonder and prate" about the news and to await Uncle William's arrival. Lucy put aside her writing and joined the anxious circle.[31]

Hours after the dew had driven Lucy and her excited kin indoors the normally tranquil McKinley was heard galloping up the road. His unaccustomed approach threw the members of his family into a second frenzy, all of them rushing out of the house to greet him. "Be quick girls and hear what I have to say," he began. "The Yankees are in ten miles of Milledgeville. They are expected at ten o'clock, may not come before morning, or at all if Genl. [Henry C.] Wayne and his men get here in time." He then exhorted the members of his household to compose themselves and listen very carefully as he explained what he had done before leaving town. Thereafter he asked them to return to the house and prepare for the worst.[32]

The worst turned out to be a total surprise. While in Milledgeville McKinley had visited the executive mansion and what he saw there touched him deeply. He found the governor's wife pale and terror striken, racing aimlessly through the house she feared would be burned before morning. With nearly all of the Brown family on her hands and no place to go, she had received within an hour three dispatches from her husband urging her to flee southward with the children. To have done so would have meant leaving behind the governor's bedfast mother and a sister-in-law with a two-months-old baby. Uncle William suddenly forgot old political feuds and invited Mrs. Brown to bring her family with "all their Cherokee plunder" to his house.[33]

When McKinley had concluded his explanation of what he saw and did at the executive mansion, his household gave him some hearty applause and then dispersed to make ready for Georgia's first family. It was Lucy's belief that Mrs. Brown could not honorably have fled southward with her children, even though commanded to do so by her husband. She was also of the opinion that the unselfishness of her uncle would bring upon his family the blessing of Heaven and "insure for us the special care and protection of Providence."[34]

As his family dispersed McKinley turned and went back to town to pack up the Browns. Soon the first carriage load reached the planter's house. Throughout the remainder of the night there was a steady procession of carriages and wagons to and from the executive mansion. By daybreak all the Browns had arrived "bag and baggage," piling the hall with luggage, sugar, coffee, syrup, and other articles which some of the McKinleys strongly suspected their guests "took from the government."[35]

While the Browns were moving in throughout the night of July 29-30, those already at the McKinley house were bundling up or concealing about their persons everything they held valuable. Lucy hid two pictures in her bosom, confessing some hours later that "sharp, shooting pains warn me . . . 'tis not advisable to let them remain there." Everything else of value she placed in a bag which would be fastened to her hoops at the first signal of alarm, hoping her person would be held inviolable.[36]

Lucy vowed that except for a moment the exciting events of July 29-30 had not frightened her. The presence of Wayne's soldiers, who were really some miles distant, reassured her, but much more comforting was the knowledge that Johnny's father was fighting the raiders at Macon. Yet her letter written to Johnny late on July 30 leaves the impression that she was deeply shocked, perhaps too shocked for fright, by the ordeal of these two days. She admitted to being lost in "an agony of dread and suspense" and complained that every nerve in her body was "bare and quivering." It was impossible for her to sleep, eat, or think. She could do nothing "but sit quite still, perfectly unnerved by the thought" that those she loved were being mowed down by "these northern demons," and she could do nothing, "not even pray." If she could only hear from Johnny! "God grant," she wrote him on July 30, "that you at least may be in Sumter."

The Browns afforded their hosts a mixture of amusement, pity, and contempt. To this extent they helped the McKinleys forget their troubles. Lucy's impressions of individual members of the governor's family are presented with both diagrams and epigrams in her letter to Johnny of July 30. In it she betrays her own mixed feelings toward the Browns. Her generous use of superlatives, it may safely be assumed, was intended to vindicate her spouse, to whom the governor had always been an unmitigated scamp. Since he was sired by one who was misshapen and himself sired so many who were misshapen, his excellency Joseph Emerson Brown was at least caught in Lucy's syllogistic trap. Never had she seen such an afflicted family. It was scarcely possible to turn around without having "some little deformed face peering from behind a corner." There was "blear-eyed Joe," the most "uncouth specimen," and Franklin Pierce, the "poor little cripple with the crooked spine, and the knot on his breast." His name, boasted Mrs. Brown, was only one of the "big" names among her children. Lucy thought he was very smart, but also very disgusting. Elijah, next in the Brown "catalogue of affliction," was, as his grandfather put it, "a little hard o' hearing." Sallie, the baby, had a breaking out which Lucy believed to be scrofulous. Vilest of all was the male Negro nurse, whose cough was consumptive and whose face bore strong evidence of scrofula.

Lucy thought the most frightening of all the Browns was the governor's father. His withered face, sagging jaws, and curious, prying look were shocking to behold. Horror stricken at the sight of him, Lucy vanished when he came into view "as if struck by a thunderbolt from Jupiter." Most bizarre of all was the governor's older sister, Mary Jane. She was a tall, gaunt maid of thirty-five. Her droopy jaws resembled those of her father and her head bore ponderous ringlets to accentuate her "girlish ways." Lucy thought the younger sister was "Joseph's self in petticoats." A strange family, at least so Lucy pictured them. Of all its members, she seems to have been convinced that only the governor's wife and his mother were normal human beings. To them she referred as "decent" and "sensible." Like the Yankees, the Brown "invaders" soon returned to their base. On August 3 Lucy wrote her husband that the danger was over and that none had been molested, by either Yankees or Browns.

CHAPTER IX

Flight From the Bear's Den

WHILE Lucy Barrow Cobb was at her Uncle William Mc-Kinley's plantation helping to make ready for a raid that never came off, her relatives and friends in Macon faced their first Yankee raiding party. On July 30 Major General George Stoneman's raiders reached the shores of the Ocmulgee River opposite Macon. There they were met by a force commanded by Major General Howell Cobb. Present during this action, known as the Battle of East Macon, were General Johnston and Governor Brown, the latter obligingly turning over to Howell the state militia. The raiders quickly discovered they could not cross the river, whereupon they turned and raced off, only to run into a Confederate Cavalry force which captured their leader and some 600 of his men.[1]

General Cobb was happy over the Battle of East Macon. He was particularly pleased to have at his side Johnston, who paid him the compliment of asserting that "by his own courage and judicious disposition" he assured victory. Brown had also behaved well, though not quite in the manner described by the friendly editor who wrote that the governor had led the troops while the other two men merely observed.[2]

Although these raids of late July 1864 were mild by comparison with what was in store for Georgia and South Carolina, yet they were nonetheless damaging. The raiders seized horses, mules, and provisions. What they could not easily carry off, they burned. Such treatment was reserved especially for factories and mills. It would appear that these visitors committed no outrages against white women, though Howell reported some cases of Negro women having been ravished in the presence of their mistresses.[3] It is not clear what damage Howell's plantations suffered at this time. One report alleged that at one of them the Yankees tried unsuccessfully to abduct the Negroes, though one small boy was said to have been stolen by them. Cobb himself was reported to have said that these raids cost him "about one hundred thousand dollars."[4] Despite the inflated currency of the time, it is difficult to accept this as a judicious estimate. Because raiders posed a wholesale threat to hearths and fields, as well as to roads and mills, they had to be prepared for the worst should captivity be their fate. Understandably, Howell favored extreme treatment. On August 7 he wrote his wife to express the hope that Colonel Andrew Young had caught the raiders who had lately been molesting the Athens area, adding: "I think it is likely *he lost them*—as is his habit with such cattle."

A few days after the July raids Lucy went to Athens to be with Mrs. Kilcrease. Within two weeks she was again back with the McKinleys and immediately found the entire Milledgeville area wrought up afresh over the threat of more raids. Startled by every unusual noise she heard, Lucy concluded the best remedy was to keep busy. Accordingly, she joined the ladies of the state capital in their daily preparation and delivery of food to the wounded soldiers in the local hospital. Lucy claimed the Commissary Department at Milledgeville was so inefficient that unless the ladies acted the soldiers would starve.[5] Johnny, however, held a contrary view of his wife's responsibility, personally escorting her to the Bear's Den on August 19.

Macon was not a pleasant place during late summer of 1864. Howell's Georgia Reserve Force headquarters was there. The Reserve's responsibility, so decisively executed on July 20 at East Macon, was to defend Georgia southward from Atlanta against the forays of Sherman's troops, the Army of Tennessee being too busy trying to halt the main Yankee thrust. Actually the Bear's Den had become a military command post second in importance to Atlanta. Leading state and Confederate officials were constantly coming and going. So crowded was it that two tents had to be put up amidst the gum trees in the back yard to accommodate transient guests.[6]

Such were the circumstances amid which Johnny was

trying to manage the widely scattered Cobb holdings with
two instead of the four or five overseers he really needed.
Little wonder that he became more irascible. Unfortunately
his wife was sometimes the victim of his fits of temper. After
an outburst remorse passed only after profuse apologies and
repeated vows of improved comportment. "If I wish to vent
my bad temper in future," he promised Lucy after what appears to have been one of his most violent outbursts that he
would "select some other person and not offend the best and
sweetest wife in the world."[7]

Lucy was deeply hurt by her cantankerous husband's
occasional eruptions, yet she was ever the understanding and
forgiving wife. "Nothing is so good for a soul aggrieved,"
she assured him after receiving one of his recantations, "as
an honest confession, *then* a desire to be forgiven, and [finally]
to have all future shortcomings overlooked, for the sake of
the great love that *should* exist between the parties." This
was exactly their case, she continued, and their "precious love"
alone must be their safeguard. "Oh! my husband, what can
harm us, so long as we bear this mantle of love about us!"[8]

Late summer and early fall brought no surcease from
troubles for Cobbs, Barrows, or Georgians in general. "Atlanta
has fallen!!" wrote Johnny to his wife on September 4, the
day after Sherman occupied the city. This disaster deepened
young Cobb's gloom and heightened his aversion for some
of the top Confederate leaders. The "prejudiced" Davis and
the "malicious" Bragg had conspired to remove the "able"
Johnston. Little wonder, he opined, that catastrophe had be-
fallen the noble cause. An outraged people would hold both
Davis and Bragg responsible; but there was really little hope
for improved leadership, he continued, for Davis was not
man enough to admit his great error in dismissing Johnston as
commander of the Army of Tennessee.

Two days before Atlanta fell Lucy left Macon for Athens
in the company of her father, Cousin Bessie, Mrs. Kilcrease,
and others. Soon after boarding the Augusta train at Gordon
Station, a short distance east of Macon, all ate heartily from
three well-filled baskets that were brought along. Then the
party dispersed to rest, if possible to sleep, for the night. Lucy
managed to find an unoccupied seat, on which she contrived

a bed of sorts. With her head toward the aisle and the open window at her feet, she fell asleep in the dimly lighted car. But she slept only briefly, for an "old tobacco chewing, country woman," believing the place vacant, seated herself firmly on Lucy's veil-covered head. After the two passengers had disencumbered themselves and their baggage, Lucy mustered enough politeness to invite her disturber to share the seat. Arriving in Augusta at dawn, Barrow took his party from the depot of the Central of Georgia to that of the Georgia Railroad. There at the pumps with the road hands Lucy "made a very decent toilet" before resuming the journey. The party reached Athens in time "to partake of a smoking hot and most tempting supper."[9]

Lucy expected to return to Macon within three weeks; but, because Johnny could not find time to go after her, she was to remain in Athens almost two months instead. Between reading and making shirts for soldiers she found much time to be with her grandmother and Mrs. Kilcrease, the widow from Quincy, who, according to Mary Ann Cobb, understood "the art of entangling men, as spiders do unwary flies."[10] There were teas and parties, which by now Lucy had come to abhor. Often she complained of loneliness, but except for the "horrid ringworms crawling over" her body, her health was good. She urged Johnny to take good care of himself, adding that if it would avail him anything "*drench* yourself in 'Custom House Brandy.'"[11]

Johnny may have tried the kind of preventive medicine his wife prescribed, but he certainly had no time for prolonged treatment. Added to his customary duties as manager of the Cobb plantations were those as procurer for Cobbs and Barrows, as well as for their friends and relatives. Indeed he had become an *avant-courier* of the twentieth century "man who can get it wholesale." He was expected to provide everything from "black bosom buttons" and bonnet boxes to a house in Americus. Howell, it will be recalled, had decided in April that his family must be removed as far as possible from the dangers of war. It became his son's responsibility to acquire a suitable house in Americus. For months the search went on. One prospect was lost when the owner changed his mind literally amid preparations to transfer the title. As Johnny had gone all the way from Macon to Americus to conclude the transaction, his disappointment is understandable. He vented his feelings on the Baptist Church of which the inconstant owner was a member, declaring if it could get such a man into the Celestial City then it could arrange to have anybody admitted. It was not until the end of September that Johnny got his house, the Willis Hawkins house, for which he paid $45,000.[12] It had nine rooms with, in the words of Mary Ann, "innumerable colonnades, piazzas, porches, passages, pantries, and closets." Five passages intersected the house, and the windows of the rooms on the passages extended to the floor. And there, she continued, "we shall be 'near the base of our supplies[the Sumter plantation]' of meat, corn, potatoes, peas, back bones, spare ribs, and sausages, so that with Heaven's smile upon us we shall have no lack and no fear of any thing."[13]

Meanwhile the military situation in Georgia was rapidly deteriorating. One newspaper reported within a week after the fall of Atlanta that deserters from Lieutenant General Joseph Wheeler's cavalry were a far greater menace to the people of Baldwin County than Sherman's raiders.[14] General John B. Hood, the unsuccessful defender of Atlanta, pulled his army southward to Lovejoy's Station, where he joined Lieutenant General William J. Hardee's corps, while Governor Brown, determined to head off the War Department's attempt to incorporate his troops into the Confederate Army, finally resolved matters by giving his "Malish" a furlough of thirty days. It was during Brown's altercation with the Confederate Secretary of War that Sherman put out peace feelers, communicating with three Georgia Unionists who he hoped would invite the governor and Vice President Alexander H. Stephens to a conference.[15]

With the Vice President and Governor Brown linked to a peace movement that might well sweep Georgia out of the war, President Davis hastened to Macon for a talk with Howell. Of all the prominent Georgians of the pre-war days, Cobb alone was widely respected for his ability to reconcile his devotion to the Confederacy with a personal dislike for its chief executive. Like Brown, Stephens had been a chronic opponent of Davis almost from the war's start, while Robert

Toombs delighted in boasting that the Confederacy would win its independence in spite of "that scoundrel Jeff Davis."[16]

When the President arrived at Macon's Central of Georgia depot at four o'clock on the morning of September 24, Howell was there to meet him and take him to the Bear's Den. While there Davis received an invitation to address a meeting that had gathered in the Baptist Church to consider means for the relief of Atlanta refugees. Shortly before noon Cobb introduced Davis to the gathering and the President made a brief speech. After a few hortative remarks he proceeded to berate the Reserve, the militia, and the soldiers of the Army of Tennessee. Two-thirds of them were not at their posts, he claimed, adding indiscreetly that if half the men "now absent without leave will return to duty, we can defeat the enemy."[17]

The President's remarks annoyed some Georgia editors, but the harassed Davis did not tarry to read their criticisms.[18] He was off in the afternoon to Palmetto, about twenty-five miles west of Lovejoy's, to visit the headquarters of the Army of Tennessee. With him were Howell and Lamar. Both the President and Howell spoke to the soldiers on the afternoon of the 26th.[19] A few days later they returned to Macon and then went on to Augusta. In the latter city they were joined by Beauregard and Hardee. After several major command problems had been decided, the President and his generals departed. Beauregard accompanied Howell as far as Gordon Station, going thence to Milledgeville to pay his respects to Governor Brown.[20] Johnny wrote Lucy that it was "a smart trick for him [Beauregard] to make a friend of Joseph I by soft soaping him a little."[21]

The "soft soaping" of Joe Brown would seem to have worked, for on October 6 he and his leading military advisers gathered at the Bear's Den to confer with Howell and Beauregard. Johnny characterized the conferees as a "gay crowd."[22] Gay it may have been; it was also exotic. In the Bear's Den was a Louisiana Creole expecting to arbitrate an Anglo-Saxon tug of war within the Confederacy, which had pitted the patrician Cobb against the plebeian Brown. The Creole was unquestionably an able general. That he understood the social compulsions which gave motion and substance to the

Brown-Cobb feud is doubtful. Contained before the war, this social struggle was unleashed by the disruption and demoralization resulting from armed conflict. Brown might be momentarily conciliated, but he must return to that contest which for a century was to be a vital force in Southern history. At this conference the governor agreed to turn over to Cobb his state militia, which probably numbered fewer than the 12,000 estimated by Beauregard.[23]

Appeasing Brown apparently did not include an invitation to help consume an immense gobbler for which Johnny had paid the fabulous sum of $35.00.[24] However, Howell and Mary Ann did accord this privilege to Beauregard and General and Mrs. Johnston.[25] All three, along with some other guests, had a gay time at what was described as "Mother's very fine dinner" by Johnny, who in "getting out wine" for the occasion had soiled his only white shirt and therefore chose to eat at the second table with "sister and the small fry." While Johnny was pleased with the events of October 6, he was also greatly upset by the extended absence of his wife; and when Mrs. Johnston inquired about her return he was embarrassed, observing in his letter to Lucy the next day: ". . . but that question I could not answer for I have not heard one word since I wrote to you that I wanted you to come down."

Busy with preparations to move the Cobbs to Americus, Johnny found it impossible to go after Lucy and on October 15 literally ordered her to return to Macon with Howell, Jr. A few days earlier he had reminded her that lately he had "given up" to her on everything and it was now her turn to grant his wish. "I have great plans for our life for this winter," he continued, though "I will not promise that Americus will be as gay as Macon was last winter. . . ."[26] When he left on the 16th for the Sumter plantation and Americus, Lucy had not yet returned from Athens. It was more than a week later that they were once more together at the Bear's Den.[27] As so often since their marriage in July 1863, they were again to be quickly separated.

After the Bear's Den conference of October 6 Howell was confronted with the knotty problem of getting the militia and Reserve absentees to return to their units. Secretary of State Judah P. Benjamin declared late in the same month that he was "shocked at the picture of depravity" in Georgia and hoped it would soon be possible "to cleanse the Augean Stable."[28] The alleged plundering of the Reserve absentees was brought to the attention of the War Department. The Secretary of War acted promptly by ordering Howell to punish the guilty parties, but he promised all who would voluntarily come forward forgiveness instead.[29] Despite the gloomy outlook, Cobb managed during the first days of November to move 10,000 to 12,000 men of a potential force of 17,000 Reserves and militia to "Camp Bald Head" near Lovejoy's Station.[30]

From "Bald Head" Johnny wrote Lucy on November 3, recording impressions of his first camp life since the Maryland campaign of September 1862. Incessant rains, no tents, thin clothing, and few blankets or overcoats was the lot of Cobb's Reserves and militiamen. "The only chance to keep life in them," wrote his son, "is to make big fires and stand by them." As an officer who was somewhat loosely attached to his father's staff, Johnny fared better; he managed to keep dry and warm. Food was also ample for staff members, Howell reporting to Mary Ann that for $10.00 he bought the biggest and fattest gobbler he had seen all year. Since it was too large for his oven, he roasted the bird by swinging him in front of a fire with one string "around his neck" and another "around the Parson's nose."[31]

Down in Macon the Cobbs were eating well too. From the plantations had come lard, a fat quarter of beef, and buckets of butter. Mary Ann wrote that she, Lucy, the youngsters, and relatives were "living upon the *fat* of the land." She also observed that the rats were becoming more numerous and much bolder. From attic, stables, and smoke house they rendezvoused at the Bear's Den; between feasts at the Cobb larder they held balls on the back stoop and parades in the first floor passage.[32] The elder Cobb was never long away from home without making a levy on the family storehouse. Whether he sent Johnny home to help prepare a shipment of his favorite foods is uncertain, but on November 10 his son was back at the Bear's Den assisting Mary Ann make ready a box containing a boiled ham, biscuits, two bottles of whiskey, one bottle of green pepper catsup, three dozen green peppers, and a string of red peppers. Displeased with Johnny's behavior, Mary Ann wrote her husband that their son was unfortunately endowed with the "Cobb love of ease and makeshift fashion of doing things."[33]

While Johnny was at the front "to see as much of what is going on . . . as possible without running any risk of life or limb," Lucy had a dream.[34] For an entire night, according to her account, she dreamed that a gallant man was making love to her. "*Don't* frown, my dear old Bluebeard," she wrote Johnny as a prelude to the conspectus of her account of the provocation. An uncle and widower, a Dr. Johnston, stopped over at the Bear's Den for several days and took a fancy to Lucy, who pictured him as a "big square shouldered Tennessean." One evening after supper he followed her and the Cobb children into the parlor and asked for music. Lucy obliged by playing and singing with her "usual *amiability*" and was rewarded by several "*love* songs" and recitations of poetry from the guest. For her the evening had been agreeable enough, except that throughout she could not drive away the miserable consciousness of an approaching sick headache. In the midst of the entertainment she rose to leave, pleading her now throbbing headache as the reason for her action. At this point the gallant widower stepped forward, apologized for having been so tiresome, and insisted upon prescribing for his ailing host. "With the gentleness of a woman," he took her aching head between his two hands. The pain quickly left, but not the magnetic touch. It lingered upon her brow to induce a "night-long dream" of the chivalrous gentleman, during which she once fancied herself in the clasp of his manly arms.

What was presently to take place north of Macon was no dream. On November 14 Beauregard ordered Howell to fall back to the city at once and prepare to defend it. The following day Atlanta was in flames and Sherman was dividing his army, ordering the left wing to Sandersville by way of Milledgeville and the right to the same destination by way of Jonesboro with instructions to simulate an attack on Macon. The Sherman crusher stormed past Macon, precipitating in its vicinity only two minor brushes. One occurred at East Macon on November 19 and the other three days later at Griswold Station. Storming through Baldwin County, the

Yankee whirlwind included among its places of call Cobb's plantation and then pushed on to the sea.[35]

A few days before Sherman's cavalry hit East Macon Johnny supervised the flight of the Cobb women and children to Americus.[36] Despite the four or five carloads of furniture that had gone ahead and the thirty-five trunks they took with them, Mary Ann wrote Howell, Jr., on November 20 to send a formidable list of items left behind. The Cobb women were settling down for what they believed would be a long absence from the Bear's Den.

Chapter X

The End

THE refugees from the Bear's Den were soon comfortably settled in their new home. Apparently the ladies of Americus were not socially inclined, only three having called on the newcomers by the time they had been in town ten days. Lucy credited them with being considerate and thought such people should be commended for staying at home and minding their own business. When at Howell's request Mary Ann returned to Macon on November 28, Lucy became the "mistress of this great house and establishment," which she thought bore upon its "very face the impress" of her mother-in-law's dignity and character. Externally it was grand and imposing; internally, "hollow and cold" at first sight, but afterwards more pleasing as time and better acquaintance brought to light its true beauty. Managing the domestic labor in such a house was itself a major responsibility, but Lucy was also charged with hearing the recitations of the younger children who were left with her and Johnny.[1] While hearth and larder held priority, intellectual endeavors were not to be abandoned.

Among the Cobbs, food had always been an object of special devotion. Howell's appetite for pork was ravenous and may be the explanation of his stomach ailment and death at age fifty-three. Mary Ann promptly took advantage of the proximity of her new home to the Sumter plantation storehouse to provide her husband with spare ribs, backbones, and sausages. An early shipment included a bucket of sausage which she hoped would be "hot enough."[2] Howell regularly ordered Johnny to provide him with pork, writing Mary Ann in January 1865 to instruct their son to "send up some [provisions] at once, sausages in particular."[3]

Despite raids by Yankees and Rebel deserters, Johnny could report in December 1864 large swine herds, seventy hogs having been brought to Sumter from the Baldwin place alone.[4] Pork was supplemented by an abundance of fish, turkeys, chickens, geese, and ducks.[5] To preserve his meat, particularly the pork, Johnny required salt. Fortunately there was a supply at the Bear's Den, but vastly more important was the Barrow salt works near St. Marks, Florida. This enterprise had not been sold, as Johnny and his father advised, nor had it "gone up the spout" during the Yankee occupation of a part of the Florida coast, as was originally feared. Instead when the Yankees left in March, the salt works, for some time a joint enterprise of Barrow and his son-in-law, was undamaged. In mid-March Johnny sent some big kettles to St. Marks, promising the works would be in production in two weeks.[6]

While the Yankees may have been less destructive along Florida's gulf coast than Sherman had been a few hundred miles northward, when the latter's army passed through central Georgia it was gone forever. There were rumors that it might return, but the real danger during the winter of 1864-65 came from deserters, absentees, and thieves. From Augusta to Macon the countryside was reported to be "full of stragglers from the cavalry commands." Their depredations brought widespread complaints from helpless citizens, and late in 1864 the *Milledgeville Confederate Union* declared that unless the government put an end to the plundering by bands masquerading as loyal soldiers, the days of the Confederacy were numbered.[7]

With Sherman gone there was no longer a need for the Cobbs to maintain their Americus home. Accordingly, Lucy and the elder Cobb children returned to the Bear's Den on February 11, and three days later "the Genl." went to Americus to hasten the departure of his wife and their two youngest children.[8] He returned next day, not with wife and children, but with a supply of eggs instead.[9] Johnny humorously observed that his father had undertaken an impossible task, yet by February 23, about three months after their flight, all the Cobbs were again at the Bear's Den. The furniture in Americus had been hauled to the depot and in April the house was sold for $70,000.[10]

No sooner had the Bear's Den again become the center of Cobb family life than once more Lucy took leave, this time to visit her Uncle William McKinley's family. As Johnny had to make his customary visits to the Baldwin place, Lucy's plan was to return with him after a short visit. Heavy rains and swollen rivers, however, were to keep her away from the Bear's Den during most of March. A helpless husband repeated his old threat that when he got his wife home again he would keep her there. "To get you back when you once get away," he lamented, was like catching a "bird that has been in a cage."[11]

Actually Lucy found herself in something of a cage at the McKinleys. She had become a captive of Rebel soldiers, "infants in arms" she called them, who literally stood in line to hear her play the piano. Often she would play for hours to a room filled with noisy soldiers. Delighted to comply with the requests of "the defenders of my country," she was amazed at their banal tastes and remarked that the piano "had got so" it acknowledged only jigs, polkas, and marches. There would be an occasional request for a Confederate ballad, usually "Who Will Care for Mother Now?" or "The Bonny Blue Flag." She remembered one soldier who had a taste of his own and called for "Billy Grimes," which he insisted was a "beautiful piece." A rollicking, sentimental Westerner named Le Vert once tormented Lucy until she played "Wake Lady Wake, Thy Harp Awaits Thee" and "The Lone Starry Hours." He was a wild, rattlebrained youngster, who imagined himself a poet and a gentleman. The son of a Methodist minister, this soldier boasted that twenty-five preachers had bet him that he would one day join them. Lucy observed that should this happen, he would have answered when "some one else was called." Two modest Irish soldiers with the "unpronounceable" name of McAdory and the qualities of saints were Lucy's favorites.[12]

Le Vert and the two Irish boys took dinner with the McKinleys one evening. Lucy's Aunt Annie, having heard the elder McAdory remark he was a church member, called on him "to ask the blessing." He declined through "sheer bashfulness," whereupon, in the judgment of Lucy, Le Vert "launched forth into what he would have done if called on" and what had unquestionably long been his customary behavior. The uninhibited soldier gave a lengthy testimonial, during which he boasted that he had once prayed in a meeting, that he had also "told his experience" in public, and that he would not refuse to respond if requested to say grace. At this point the dinner was threatened by May McKinley's interruption to rebuke Le Vert, gravely charging him with mockery. Lucy did not share her cousin's severe judgment of the young man, but she was astonished that "he ever kept his face straight long enough to do such things with becoming sobriety."[13]

That his wife should heed the demands of the "infants in arms" bothered Johnny. "You may not fret it," he protested after returning to the Bear's Den on March 12, "but it is too great an exertion for you, playing so constantly. . . ." A patronizing husband was confident his wife would grant him his wish, because "I know you prefer pleasing me to pleasing them."[14] His anxiety may have been heightened by fear of a miscarriage, for a few weeks later, when it was certain that Lucy was pregnant, he cautioned her to be "more prudent in future for fear our cherished hope long delayed, may travel the way of its predecessor."[15]

An anxious husband, bearing thirteen partridges, expected to surprise his wife as he returned to the Bear's Den from Sumter on March 12. Instead he discovered she had not yet come home. Of Howell, Jr., recently at the McKinleys paying court to May, Johnny inquired about Lucy's health. It was a futile request, the suitor proving oblivious to all others but his darling and replying with monumental egocentrism that she was well, the river was high, and he had been compelled to walk a great distance in the mud. But the river was to recede and Lucy was soon to be back with her husband.[16]

Meanwhile Federal troops were driving eastward across Alabama, and to General Howell Cobb had fallen the responsibility of turning them back at the Georgia border. By this time many Georgians had lost the will to resist. Deserters continued to harass helpless citizens who in desperation cried out for peace. Even President Davis admitted as early as January that nearly all wished an end to the war.[17] The fall of Richmond in early April dealt a crushing blow to those

who had hoped for indefinite resistance. Across the Chattahoochee River, Selma, Alabama, had also fallen, and Johnny
wrote his wife on April 6 that Mobile and Montgomery would
likely suffer the same fate. But, he hopefully continued,
"while things look gloomy, . . . 'the darkest hour precedes
the dawn.'" With Johnston restored to command, he and
Lee would yet save the situation in Virginia, while Lieutenant
General Richard Taylor would drive the enemy from Alabama. Such were the blind hopes of Howell's oldest son,
hopes he admitted could be realized only if the soldiers acted
well and the people back home ceased their complaints and
"talk of peace on any terms." But Johnny had really not
been mesmerized; like so many others, he too had abandoned
hope of victory. Just when he had done so cannot be determined, but near the end of his letter of April 6 he probably
expressed his true feelings when he wrote: "I hope in any new
movements that are made that Ga. will not become the
'Theater of War.'"

Such was the state of affairs during the second week in
April, as Howell prepared to stop Major General J. H. Wilson
at Columbus on the Georgia side of the Chattahoochee River.
On April 17 the city fell, Cobb escaping to Macon with about
600 men. On the 20th, eleven days after Lee's surrender at
Appomattox, Howell received a dispatch from Beauregard
announcing an armistice. Later that day he surrendered to
Wilson. Thus four years to the day after Johnny had left
the Bear's Den for Virginia the war ended.[18]

For Johnny and Lucy these four years had been a time of
love, devotion, bitter grief, and sweet resignation. During the
five weeks that followed Howell's surrender it was to be
the lot of the young couple again to endure all of these emotions. Late in May the elder Cobb was arrested in Athens,
Lucy writing Johnny from there that the Federal officers
"have done nothing to make the bare fact more galling and
humiliating than it necessarily is."[19] When "the Genl." was
taken away on the following day as a prisoner Lucy's resignation turned to compassion for him and bitterness for his
captors. "Oh!" cried an anguished conscience, "Is it possible
to have one feeling of kindness for these vile wretches who
have so ruthlessly desolated our homes and torn our hearts?"[20]

From "such sacrilege" she speedily asked heaven's protection, and was able the next day to feel that "the Genl. was treated with great *courtesy* and *consideration*" by the guard which took him away.[21] Her husband could likewise reflect that the "kind treatment" shown his father was good evidence that the United States government was at least not as bitter toward him as toward some others it had arrested.[22] With characteristic joviality, the prisoner's parting message for his oldest son was that he be instructed "to go on with the business" as he had always done.[23]

Notes

CHAPTER I

1. Cobb had been in the House of Representatives, serving as speaker of the 31st Congress; in 1851 he was elected governor of Georgia and in 1857 became Secretary of the Treasury. See Horace Montgomery, *Howell Cobb's Confederate Career* (Tuscaloosa, 1959); *Americus Times-Recorder*, Jan. 5, 1910.

2. March 5, 1861. Unless otherwise indicated, this and other letters cited hereinafter are in the Howell Cobb Papers, University of Georgia Library, Athens, Ga.

3. Lamar Cobb to John A. Cobb, April 19, 1861; John A. Cobb to his mother, April 23, 1861; *Milledgeville Federal Union*, April 23, 1861.

4. Lamar Cobb to his mother [n.d.]; John A. Cobb to John B. Lamar, May 12; *id*. to his father, May 22, 1861.

5. *Id*. to John B. Lamar, April 27, May 12, July 10; *id*. to his mother, May 3, 1861; [?] to Mrs. Howell Cobb, Aug. 6, 1861.

6. Lamar Cobb to his mother, Sept. 8, 1858.

7. Oct. [n.d.], 1861; John A. Cobb to his mother, Dec. 1, 1861.

8. July 10, 1861.

9. John A. Cobb to his mother, June 16, 1861.

10. *Id*. to John B. Lamar, June 27, 1861; *id*. to *id*., Aug. 1, 17, 28, Sept. 8, 1861; Lamar Cobb to *id*., Aug. 22, 1861; *id*. to his father, Aug. 2, 1861; John A. Cobb to John B. Lamar, Aug. 28, 1861.

11. *Id*. to *id*., Sept. 8, 1861.

12. *Id*. to *id*., Sept. 12, 1861; *War of the Rebellion* . . . (Washington, 1880-1901), 1 Ser., XI, Pt. 1, 406 (hereinafter cited ORA).

13. Ezra J. Warner, *Generals in Gray* (Baton Rouge, 1959), 207-08. Howell Cobb wrote his wife from Camp Bryan late in 1861 that Magruder "is a prudent, wise and brave officer." He characterized as a "gross slander" the "rumor that he drinks and is reckless and impulsive." Cobb to his wife [n.d.].

14. John A. Cobb to John B. Lamar, Sept. 12, Oct. 6, 1861; Robert A. Smith to Lamar Cobb, Sept. 9, 1861; Montgomery, *Howell Cobb's Confederate Career*, 36-37.

15. William Joseph Hardee, *U. S. Rifle and Light Infantry Tactics* (New York, 1856).

16. Barrow had entered the United States Military Academy at West Point in July 1858, and early in 1861 he resigned.

17. John A. Cobb to his mother, Oct. 14, 1861.

87

18. *Athens Southern Banner*, Nov. 6, 1861; John A. Cobb to John B. Lamar, Oct. 21, 27, 1861.

19. *Id.* to *id.*, Oct. 23, 27, 1861.

20. T. R. R. Cobb's Legion was stationed three miles to the south of Camp Bryan. On Dec. 12, 1861, Johnny wrote his mother that Howell, Jr., had arrived on the Peninsula the day before.

21. John A. Cobb to John B. Lamar, Oct. 27, 1861.

22. *Id.* to his mother, Dec. 1, 12, 1861; *id.* to John B. Lamar, Jan. 1, 1862.

23. Mrs. Howell Cobb to John A. Cobb, Dec. 8, 29, 1861.

24. John A. Cobb to John B. Lamar, Dec. 16, 1861.

25. Mrs. Howell Cobb to John A. Cobb, Dec. 29, 1861.

CHAPTER II

1. E. Merton Coulter, *Lost Generation: The Life and Death of James Barrow, C. S. A.* (Tuscaloosa, 1956), 13-15. Barrow owned a plantation of 4,500 acres near Athens. He also maintained a home in Athens.

2. *Athens Southern Banner*, Feb. 2, 1860.

3. This letter has not been seen, but on its anniversary Johnny referred to it. John A. Cobb to Lucy Barrow, Feb. 1, 1863, in possession of Lucy Taylor Bucknell, Bluemont, Virginia. Numerous other references were made to it by Lucy and her brother James.

4. Lucy Barrow to John A. Cobb, Feb. 25, 1862.

5. April 13, 1861, in possession of Lucy Taylor Bucknell.

6. James Barrow to John A. Cobb, Feb. 6, 1862, in possession of Lucy Taylor Bucknell.

7. John A. Cobb to his mother, March [n.d.], 1862; *id.* to John B. Lamar, March 17, 1862; Howell Cobb to *id.*, Feb. 22, March 17, 1862; John A. Cobb to Howell Cobb, Jr., March 23, 1862; *id.* to his mother, April 1, 1862; ORA, 1 Ser., IX, 449.

8. John A. Cobb to John B. Lamar, April 6, 1862.

9. ORA, 1 Ser., XI, Pt. 3, 425.

10. Cobb's report, April 22, 1862; Cobb to his wife, April 18, 1862.

11. John A. Cobb to his mother, April 24, 1862; Montgomery, *Howell Cobb's Confederate Career*, 58.

12. Howell Cobb to his wife, May 26, 1862; ORA, 1 Ser., XI, Pt. 3, 229-30, 530-31.

13. George B. McClellan, *McClellan's Own Story* (New York, 1887), 385; Robert Underwood Johnson and Clarence Clough Buel, eds., *Battles and Leaders of the Civil War* (New York, 1887), II, 323-24.

14. Lucy Barrow to John A. Cobb, June 29, 1862; John A. Cobb to Lucy Barrow, July 6, 1862.

15. Lucy Barrow to John A. Cobb, June 29, 1862.

16. July 4, 1862; ORA, 1 Ser., XI, Pt. 2, 505, 979.

17. *Macon* (Ga.) *Telegraph*, July 22, 1862. Thomas R. R. Cobb wrote his wife (Sept. 1, 1862) that the surgeons "drink up all the brandy and whiskey furnished for the sick, neglect their patients and crown it all by lying about it."

18. John A. Cobb to Lucy Barrow, July 6, 1862; Thomas R. R. (Tom) Cobb to his wife, July 8, 1862; Howell Cobb's furlough orders, July 12, 1862.

19. John A. Cobb to John B. Lamar, July 31, 1862.

CHAPTER III

1. Coulter, *Lost Generation*, 69.
2. Ms. in Cobb Papers.
3. Lucy Barrow to John A. Cobb, Sept. 7, 1862.
4. Warner, *Generals in Gray*, 204-05; Montgomery, *Howell Cobb's Confederate Career*, 75-76.
5. Howell Cobb to his wife, Aug. 19, 1862; John A. Cobb to Lucy Barrow, Aug. 18, 1862.
6. T. Harry Williams, *Lincoln and His Generals* (New York, 1952), 144-52.
7. With McLaws' Division were D. H. Hill's and John G. Walker's. See Douglas Southall Freeman, *Lee's Lieutenants: A Study in Command*, (New York, 1945), II, 145.
8. John A. Cobb to Lucy Barrow, Aug. 23, 1862.
9. Lucy Barrow to John A. Cobb, Aug. 31, 1862.
10. *Athens Southern Banner*, July 8, 1858, Dec. 25, 1861; George White, *Statistics of the State of Georgia* (Savannah, 1849), 406.
11. John A. Cobb to Lucy Barrow, Aug. 15, 1862.
12. Lucy Barrow to John A. Cobb, Aug. 31, Sept. 2, 1862.
13. *Ibid*.
14. John A. Cobb to James Barrow, Aug. 24, 1862; *id.* to Lucy Barrow, Aug. 25, 28, 1862.
15. Warner, *Generals in Gray*, 136-37.
16. For an account of the Toombs-Hill trouble see U. B. Phillips, *The Life of Robert Toombs* (New York, 1913), 244.
17. John A. Cobb to Lucy Barrow, Aug. 28, 1862.
18. *Ibid.;* Howell Cobb to his wife, Aug. 29, 1862.
19. John A. Cobb to Lucy Barrow, Sept. 4, 5, 1862. Howell Cobb once admitted to his wife that he had gone to war to look after his three sons.
20. John A. Cobb to Lucy Barrow, Sept. 4, 5, 6, 1862.
21. See Freeman, *Lee's Lieutenants*, II, 141, for a discussion of losses at the Second Battle of Bull Run. See ORA, 1 Ser., XLII, Pt. 1, p. 136, Pt. 3, pp. 161-62, for losses of a Union army Negro company whose captain claimed it suffered greater losses than any other Union army company reported losing in a single charge. See also Horace Montgomery, "A Union Officer's Recollections of the Negro as a Soldier," *Pennsylvania History*, XXVIII, 177.
22. John A. Cobb to Lucy Barrow, Sept. 4, 5, 6, 1862.
23. Ironically, failure to exercise the kind of precaution Johnny observed on September 4 resulted in an unhappy event on September 12. On that day Major General D. H. Hill lost one of General Lee's important dispatches. Picked up the next day by an Indiana private, it reached General McClellan. Its contents confirmed the Union general's intelligence and thereby helped doom the Maryland invasion. For an account of Lee's Lost Order see Johnson and Buel, eds., *Battles and Leaders of the Civil War*, II, 603.
24. Lucy Barrow to John A. Cobb, Sept. 7, 1862; Mrs. Howell Cobb to her son John, Sept. 8, 1862.
25. Lucy Barrow to John A. Cobb, Sept. 7, 18, 1862.
26. Cobb's Report of the Battle of Crampton's Gap.
27. ORA, 1 Ser., XIX, Pt. 1, 827.

28. Aurelia Austin, ed., "A Georgia Boy With 'Stonewall' Jackson: The Letters of James Thomas Thomson," *The Virginia Magazine of History and Biography*, LXX, 330.

29. ORA, 1 Ser., XIX, Pt. 1, 812.

30. Lucy Taylor Bucknell to the author, Nov. 12, 1962. Mrs. Bucknell, granddaughter of John A. Cobb, recalls that her grandfather once told her that had he known how to stop the bleeding he might have saved his uncle's life.

31. Howell Cobb to his wife, September 17, 24, 1862. The fighting in the gaps of South Mountain and General "Stonewall" Jackson's capture of Harpers Ferry preceded the mighty Battle of Antietam on September 17. Howell Cobb did not participate in this battle. On that day he wrote his wife from Charlestown, Virginia, that he would join his command on the 17th, or the next day. Remnants of the Second Brigade saw action on the 17th. See also ORA, 1 Ser., XXIX, Pt. 1, 857. 870-71; Freeman, *Lee's Lieutenants*, II, 209 n. 14.

32. Howell Cobb to LaFayette McLaws, Sept. 24, 1862, McLaws Papers in the University of North Carolina Library, Chapel Hill, N. C. LaFayette McLaws to Howell Cobb, Sept. 25, 1862, *ibid*.

33. Howell Cobb to his wife, Nov. 1, 1862.

34. John A. Cobb to his father, Oct. 3, 1862. Browne had been editor of the *Washington Constitution*, which acted as the "Administration organ" during the presidency of James Buchanan. Like Cobb, he became a rabid secessionist after the election of Lincoln.

35. John A. Cobb to his father, Oct. 3, 1862; Lamar Cobb to his father, Oct. 26, 1862; Montgomery, *Howell Cobb's Confederate Career*, 76.

36. Lamar Cobb to his father, Oct. 26, 1862; ORA, 1 Ser., LIII, 262; *Athens Southern Banner*, Oct. 29, 1862.

37. Howell Cobb to his wife, Nov. 1, 1862. There were now four plantations, one in each of the following counties: Baldwin, Bibb, Sumter, and Worth. The Jefferson County place had been given up.

38. Enclosure with Mrs. Howell Cobb to her husband, Jan. [?], 1863.

CHAPTER IV

1. John A. Cobb to his father, Dec. 20, 1862, R. P. Brooks, ed., in "Howell Cobb Papers," *Georgia Historical Quarterly*, VI, 361-63. At this time Cobb owned other property, but John B. Lamar had not shared in its management. Early in 1862, Johnny estimated the Cobb plantations which he was managing to be worth approximately $650,000. *Id*. to his father, Feb. 11, 1863.

2. *Id*. to his brother, Oct. 6, 1862, in possession of Lucy Taylor Bucknell.

3. *Id*. to Lucy Barrow, Oct. 8, 1862.

4. Lucy Barrow to John A. Cobb, Oct. 12, Nov. 9, Dec. 4, 1862.

5. Coulter, *Lost Generation*, 12, n. 2; Lucy Barrow to John A. Cobb, Oct. 12, 1862.

6. *Ibid.*; John A. Cobb to Lucy Barrow, Oct. 16, 1862.

7. *Ibid*.

8. *Id*. to *id*., Oct. 28, 1862.

9. *Id*. to *id*., Oct. 16, 1862.

10. *Ibid*.

11. *Id*. to *id*., Oct. 28, 1862.

12. Lucy Barrow to John A. Cobb, Nov. 9, 1862.

13. John A. Cobb to his mother, Oct. 29, 1862; Howell Cobb to his wife, Nov. 1, 1862.

14. Lucy Barrow to John A. Cobb, Dec. 7, 1862.

15. John A. Cobb to Lucy Barrow, Nov. 30, 1862; Montgomery, *Howell Cobb's Confederate Career*, 78.

16. Coulter, *Lost Generation*, 39-40; Montgomery, *Howell Cobb's Confederate Career*, 89; Lucy Barrow to John A. Cobb, Dec. 4, 7, 1862.

17. *Id.* to *id.*, Jan. 20, 1863; John A. Cobb to Lucy Barrow, Jan. 11, 1863.

18. *Id.* to *id.* Jan. 11, 26, 1863. The Cobbs often referred to the cozy relationship between the elder members of the family and General Lee. This may have been encouraged by the fact that Howell Cobb was one of the first prominent Confederates to predict a brilliant future for Lee. See Freeman, *Lee's Lieutenants*, II, 329n., and Montgomery, *Howell Cobb's Confederate Career*, 52.

19. Letter in possession of Lucy Taylor Bucknell.

20. *Ibid.*

21. John A. Cobb to Lucy Barrow, Feb. 10, March 3, 1863; *id.* to his mother, March 9, 1863.

22. March 3, 1863.

23. *Ibid.*; John A. Cobb to his mother, March 9, 1863; *id.* to Lucy Barrow, March 3, 1863.

CHAPTER V

1. Howell Cobb to Lamar Cobb, March 25, 1863; John A. Cobb to his father, April 11, 1863.

2. *Id.* to Lucy Barrow, April 21, 1863.

3. *Ibid.*

4. Lucy Barrow to John A. Cobb, May 30, 1863.

5. John A. Cobb to Lucy Barrow, May 30, 1863.

6. Lucy Barrow to John A. Cobb, June 14, 1863.

7. John A. Cobb to Lucy Barrow, April 26, 1863, in possession of Lucy Taylor Bucknell.

8. *Id.* to his mother, March 9, May 14, 1863; *id.* to his father, March 10; Howell Cobb to John A. Cobb, June 8, 1863.

9. John A. Cobb to Lucy Barrow, April 28, 1863.

10. Howell Cobb to his wife, March 11, 1863; John A. Cobb to his father, March 11, 15, 1863.

11. *Id.* to his father, March 11, 1863.

12. *Id.* to *id.*, May 7, 11, 1863.

13. *Id.* to *id.*, May 7, 11, 31, 1863.

14. Howell Cobb to John A. Cobb, July 6, 1863.

15. *Id.* to *id.*, March 25, May 11, July 6, 1863.

16. John A. Cobb to Lucy Barrow, June 7, 25, July 1, 1863.

17. *Id.* to *id.*, July 10, 1863.

18. June 25, 1863.

19. Lucy Barrow to John A. Cobb, July 8, 1863.

20. *Id.* to *id.*, June 14, 1863.

21. *Id.* to *id.*, July 8, 1863.

22. John A. Cobb to Lucy Barrow, July 10, 1863.

23. July 17, 1863.

24. July 15, 1863.

25. Lucy Taylor Bucknell, granddaughter of John A. Cobb and Lucy Barrow Cobb, recalls that her mother wrote that the marriage took place "in one of the beautiful old fashioned columned houses on Prince Ave. The house was built by Col. Richard Taylor." Lucy Taylor Bucknell to the author, March 8, 1963.

CHAPTER VI

1. John A. Cobb to his wife, Aug. 12, 1863.

2. Lucy Barrow Cobb to her husband, Aug. 12, 1863.

3. The Negroes were wanted to help with the defense of Savannah. Johnny informed his father he would send none until compelled to do so. John A. Cobb to his father, Aug. 9, 1863.

4. Montgomery, *Howell Cobb's Confederate Career*, 95.

5. Mrs. Howell Cobb to her husband, Aug. 7, 1863.

6. John A. Cobb to his father, Aug. 13, 1863.

7. Cobb had four sons at this time. Andrew was but a child; John was perhaps technically still in the Confederate military service after he became manager of the plantations, though there was uncertainty as to his status.

8. John A. Cobb to his wife, Sept. 8, 1863.

9. Horace Montgomery, ed., *Georgians in Profile: Historical Essays in Honor of Ellis Merton Coulter* (Athens, 1958), 235.

10. John A. Cobb to his wife, Sept. 8, 1863.

11. *Atlanta Confederacy*, Sept. 13, 1863; ORA, 4 Ser., II, 818, I Ser., XXVIII, Pt. 2, 348-49.

12. John A. Cobb to his wife, Sept. 13, 1863.

13. *Id.* to *id.*, Sept. 8, 1863.

14. *Id.* to *id.*, Sept. 11, 1863; Stancil Barwick to John A. Cobb, Sept. 30, 1863.

15. John A. Cobb to his wife, Sept. 11, 1863.

16. *Id.* to *id.*, Oct. 10, 1863.

17. J. T. Pelot to John A. Cobb, Sept. 29, 1863.

18. John A. Cobb to his wife, Sept. 11, 1863.

19. *Id.* to *id.*, Oct. 10, 1863.

20. *Ibid.*

21. Lucy Barrow Cobb to her husband, Aug. 12, 1863; *id.* to Mrs. Howell Cobb, Sept. 24, 1863.

22. *Ibid.*; Lucy Barrow Cobb to her brother, Sept. 23, 1863.

23. Lucy Barrow Cobb to Mrs. Howell Cobb, Sept. 24, 1863.

24. Howell Cobb to Colonel W. R. Wright, Sept. 25, 1863, Cobb's Letter Book, University of Georgia Library; Howell Cobb to his wife, Sept. 30, 1863.

25. *Id.* to *id.*, Oct. 8, 1863.

26. Mrs. Howell Cobb to her husband, Oct. 2, 1863.

27. *Ibid.*

28. *Ibid.*

29. Mrs. Howell Cobb to her husband, Oct. 8, 1863; John A. Cobb to his

wife, Oct. 10, 1863; Lucy Barrow Cobb to her father, Nov. 16, 1863, in possession of Lucy Taylor Bucknell.

30. John A. Cobb to his wife, Oct. 13, 1863.

31. Howell Cobb to his wife, Oct. 8, 1863.

32. John A. Cobb to his wife, Oct. 10, 26, Nov. 5, 1863.

33. *Ibid.*

34. John A. Cobb to his wife, Nov. 5, 6, 1863.

35. Letter in possession of Lucy Taylor Bucknell.

CHAPTER VII

1. Lucy Barrow Cobb to her father, Dec. 5, 1863, in David Crenshaw Barrow Papers, University of Georgia Library.

2. Mrs. Howell Cobb to her husband, Nov. 26, 1863.

3. P. F. Sawyer to Lucy Barrow Cobb, Nov. 23, 1863; John A. Cobb to David Crenshaw Barrow, Nov. 24, 1863, in David Crenshaw Barrow Papers.

4. Lucy Barrow Cobb to her father, Dec. 5, 1863, *ibid.*

5. Mrs. Howell Cobb to her husband, Jan. 11, 1864.

6. Howell Cobb to his wife, Nov. 28, 1863.

7. J. D. Collins to John A. Cobb, Dec. 22, 1863; Mrs. Howell Cobb to her son, Jan. 21, 1864.

8. John A. Cobb to David Crenshaw Barrow, Nov. 24, Dec. 23, 31, 1863, in David Crenshaw Barrow Papers.

9. Mrs. Howell Cobb to her husband, Jan. 11, 22, 1864.

10. *Ibid.*

11. A. R. Lawton to Maj. Gen. Howell Cobb, Dec. 3, 1863.

12. Howell Cobb to Jefferson Davis, Jan. 18, 1864, in Keith Read Collection, University of Georgia Library; Mrs. Cobb to her husband, Jan. 22, 1864.

13. John A. Cobb to his father, Jan. 23, 1864.

14. *Ibid.*

15. Mrs. Howell Cobb to her husband, Jan. 22, 1864.

16. Jan. 21, 1864.

17. John A. Cobb to his father, Jan. 23, 1864.

18. Howell Cobb to his wife, Nov. 27, 1863.

19. *Id.* to *id.*, Nov. 28, 1864.

20. *Id* to *id.*, Dec. 15, 17, 1863.

21. Mrs. Howell Cobb to her husband, Nov. 29, 1863.

22. John A. Cobb to David Crenshaw Barrow, Dec. 31, 1863, in David Crenshaw Papers.

23. *Milledgeville Daily Confederate* quoted in *Athens Southern Banner*, Jan. 27, 1864.

24. Lucy Barrow Cobb to her father, Dec. 5, 1863, in David Crenshaw Barrow Papers; Grandma Pope to Lucy Barrow Cobb, Dec. 13, 1863.

25. John A. Cobb to David Crenshaw Barrow, Dec. 23, 1863, in David Crenshaw Barrow Papers; Henry Barrow to Lucy Barrow Cobb, Jan. 1, 1864; Howell Cobb to his wife, Jan. 20, 1864.

26. John A. Cobb to David Crenshaw Barrow, Dec. 23, 31, 1863, in David Crenshaw Barrow Papers; *id* to his father, Feb. 4, 1864.

27. ORA, 1 Ser., XXVIII, Pt. 2, 15, 16, 577, 604.

28. Coulter, *Lost Generation*, 91-93.

29. In David Crenshaw Barrow Papers.

30. *Athens Southern Banner*, March 16, 1864.

31. John A. Cobb to his father, Feb. 25, 1864.

32. Lucy Barrow Cobb to Tom Barrow, March 1, 1864, in David Crenshaw Barrow Papers.

33. *Ibid.*

34. Lucy Barrow Cobb to her husband, March 4, 1864.

35. *Id.* to *id.*, March 10, 1864.

36. *Id.* to *id.*, March 12, 16, 1864.

CHAPTER VIII

1. John A. Cobb to his wife, March 3, 1864.

2. Lucy Barrow Cobb to her husband, March 10, 12, 1864; *id.* to Tom Barrow, March 10, 1864, in David Crenshaw Barrow Papers.

3. John A. Cobb to his wife, March 8, May 29, 1864.

4. Lucy Barrow Cobb to her husband, March 4, 1864.

5. John A. Cobb to his wife, March 8, 1864.

6. Lucy Barrow Cobb to her husband, March 10, 1864.

7. *Id.* to *id.*, March 12, 1864.

8. John A. Cobb to his wife, March 3, 1864.

9. Lucy Barrow Cobb to her husband, June 2, 1864.

10. Howell Cobb, Jr., to his mother, March 22, 1864; John A. Cobb to David Crenshaw Barrow, April 8, 1864, in David Crenshaw Barrow Papers.

11. *Id.* to his wife, April 18, 1864.

12. Montgomery, *Howell Cobb's Confederate Career*, 99-116.

13. *Ibid.*, 121-22.

14. John A. Cobb to his wife, April 18, 20, 1864; Lucy Barrow Cobb to Mrs. Howell Cobb, April 24, 1864.

15. *Id.* to her father, May 4, 1864, in David Crenshaw Barrow Papers.

16. *Ibid.*

17. May 24, 1864.

18. Johnson and Buel, *Battles and Leaders*, IV, 127.

19. Lucy Barrow Cobb to her father, May 4, 1864, in David Crenshaw Barrow Papers.

20. *Ibid.*

21. John A. Cobb to his wife, May 29, 1864; Lucy Barrow Cobb to her husband, June 2, 1864.

22. *Ibid.*

23. Lucy Barrow Cobb to her husband, June 6, 1864.

24. John A. Cobb to David Crenshaw Barrow, June 4, 1864, in David Crenshaw Barrow Papers.

25. To John A. Cobb, June 18, 1864.

26. Montgomery, *Howell Cobb's Confederate Career*, 121.

27. John A. Cobb to his wife, June 5, 1864; T. Conn Bryan, *Confederate Georgia* (Athens, 1953), 89; E. M. Coulter, *A Short History of Georgia* (Chapel Hill, 1958), 311.

28. John A. Cobb to to his wife, July 28, 1864.

29. *Ibid.*

30. Lucy Barrow Cobb to her husband, July 29, 1864.

31. *Ibid.*

32. *Ibid.*

33. *Ibid.* The Browns were from the hills of north Georgia, often referred to as the Cherokee Country.

34. Lucy Barrow Cobb to her husband, July 30, 1864.
35. *Ibid.*
36. *Ibid.*

CHAPTER IX

1. *Athens Southern Banner*, Aug. 10, 1864; ORA, 1 Ser., XXXVIII, Pt. 3, 689-96; Johnson and Buel, *Battles and Leaders*, IV, 342; "Official Report of the Battle of East Macon," in Cobb Papers.
2. Montgomery, *Howell Cobb's Confederate Career*, 123.
3. Howell Cobb to his wife, Aug. 3, 1864.
4. Sarah Rootes Cobb to Sarah Prince, July 25, 1864, Jackson-Prince Papers, University of North Carolina Library.
5. Lucy Barrow Cobb to her husband, Aug. 9, 12, 1864.
6. *Ibid.*
7. Sept. 4, 1864.
8. Aug. 9, 1864.
9. Lucy Barrow Cobb to her husband, Sept. 5, 6, 1864.
10. Mrs. Howell Cobb to her husband, Nov. 13, 1864.
11. Lucy Barrow Cobb to her husband, Sept. 13, 1864.
12. Howell Cobb, Jr., to his mother, Sept. 18, 1864; John A. Cobb to his wife, Sept. 11, 14, 20, 26, 28, 30, 1864.
13. Mrs. Howell Cobb to Howell, Jr., Oct. 23, 1864.
14. *Milledgeville Confederate Union*, Sept. 6, 1864.
15. Coulter, *Short History of Georgia*, 321-22; Bryan, *Confederate Georgia*, 163-64.
16. *Athens Southern Watchman*, March 2, 1864; for Toombs' views of Davis see Ulrich B. Phillips, ed., *The Correspondence of Robert Toombs, Alexander H. Stephens, and Howell Cobb* (Washington, 1913), 592, 595, 608, 611.
17. Quoted in *Milledgeville Confederate Union*, Oct. 4, 1864.
18. *Ibid.*, Oct. 11, 1864; *Augusta Weekly Chronicle and Sentinel*, Oct. 5, 1864.
19. ORA, 1 Ser., XXXIX, Pt. 1, 803-08; John A. Cobb to his wife Sept. 26, 1864.
20. *Athens Southern Banner*, Oct. 12, 1864; T. Harry Williams, *P.G.T. Beauregard: Napoleon in Gray* (Baton Rouge, 1954), 241.
21. Oct. 6, 1864.
22. John A. Cobb to his wife, Oct. 7, 1864.
23. ORA, 1 Ser., XLIV, 931-33. Brown estimated half this number.
24. John A. Cobb to his wife, Oct. 7, 1864.
25. The Johnstons had apparently remained in Macon since the general was relieved of his command. They were therefore in the city while Davis was there. On September 28 Johnny wrote Lucy that his mother went with the Johnstons house-hunting, they having learned the day before that a "negro trader" from Atlanta had rented the house they were living in and wanted it three days later.
26. Oct. 9, 1864.
27. Mrs. Howell Cobb to Howell, Jr., Oct. 23, 1864.
28. Judah P. Benjamin to William B. Browne, Oct. 29, 1864.
29. Letter Book of General Cobb, 1863-1865, No. 55, University of Georgia Library.

30. ORA, 1 Ser., XXXIX, Pt. 3, 821, 911; *ibid.*, XLIV, 54, 362-67, 861-63, 931-33.

31. Howell Cobb to his wife, Nov. 6, 1864.

32. Mrs. Howell Cobb to her husband, Nov. 7, 1864.

33. Nov. 10, 1864; Lucy Barrow Cobb to her sister, Nov. 10, 1864, David Crenshaw Barrow Papers.

34. John A. Cobb to his wife, Nov. 3, 1864; Lucy Barrow Cobb to her husband, Nov. 6, 1864.

35. ORA, 1 Ser., XLIV, 362-67, 406, 866; Howell Cobb to his wife, Nov. 24, 1864; Lucy Barrow Cobb to Cousin Bessie, Nov. 28, 1864, in David Crenshaw Barrow Papers.

36. Pope Barrow to Betsy Barrow, Nov. 20, 1864, *ibid.*

CHAPTER X

1. Lucy Barrow Cobb to her father and to Cousin Bessie, Nov. 28, 1864, in David Crenshaw Barrow Papers.

2. Mrs. Howell Cobb to her husband, Nov. 25, 1864.

3. Jan. 31, 1865, in Phillips, ed., *Correspondence*, 659.

4. John A. Cobb to his father, Dec. 18, 1864, in possession of Lucy Taylor Bucknell.

5. John A. Cobb to his wife, Feb. 15, 1865.

6. *Id.* to David Crenshaw Barrow, Dec. 29, 1864, in David Crenshaw Barrow Papers; *id.* to his wife, March 13, 14, 15, 1865. Pope Barrow, on leave in Quincy, went from there to St. Marks as a private in an artillery company and took part in the engagement which resulted in the expulsion of the Yankees. John Cobb reported that most of the Yankee soldiers were Negroes.

7. Dec. 27, 1864; Report of B. D. Fry, Dec. 16, 1864, in Cobb Papers.

8. Lucy Barrow Cobb to her sister, Feb. 14, 1865, in possession of Lucy Taylor Bucknell.

9. John A. Cobb to his wife, Feb. 15, 1864.

10. Howell Cobb, Jr., to his mother, Feb. 23, 1865; John A. Cobb to his wife, April 6, 7, 1865.

11. *Id.* to *id.*, March 13, 1865.

12. Lucy Barrow Cobb to her husband, March 6, 1865.

13. *Ibid.*

14. John A. Cobb to his wife, March 13, 1865.

15. *Id.* to *id.*, April 6, 1865.

16. *Id.* to *id.*, March 13, 14, April 6, 1865.

17. B. F. White to Lamar Cobb, Jan. 6, 1865; T. T. Dorough to Howell Cobb, March 11, 1865; Duncan L. Clinch to Howell Cobb, April 4, 1865; *Athens Southern Banner*, Feb. 15, 1865; Letter Book of General Cobb, 1865, No. 59; ORA, 1 Ser., LIII, 393-94.

18. Montgomery, *Howell Cobb's Confederate Career*, 131-32.

19. Lucy Barrow Cobb to her husband, May 23, 1865.

20. *Id.* to *id.*, May 24, 1865.

21. *Id.* to *id.*, May 25, 1865.

22. John A. Cobb to his wife, May 28, 1865.

23. Lucy Barrow Cobb to her husband, May 24, 1865.

Bibliographical Notes

THREE collections of letters furnished most of the information contained in this work: the privately-owned Howell Cobb Papers, also known as the Erwin Collection, Athens, Georgia; the David Crenshaw Barrow Papers in the University of Georgia Library; and numerous letters in possession of Lucy Taylor Bucknell of Bluemont, Virginia. Most of the letters extant that were exchanged by John A. Cobb and Lucy Barrow are in these collections. Numerous other sources have been helpful, including the University of Georgia's Keith Read Collection and two collections at the University of North Carolina: the Jackson-Prince Papers and the LaFayette McLaws Papers. Bits of pertinent data were found in the following: Ulrich B. Phillips, ed., *The Correspondence of Robert Toombs, Alexander H. Stephens, and Howell Cobb* (Washington, 1913); Robert Preston Brooks, ed., "Howell Cobb Papers," *Georgia Historical Quarterly*, V-VI (September-December, 1922); and Aurelia Austin, ed., "A Georgia Boy With 'Stonewall' Jackson: The Letters of James Thomas Thomson," *The Virginia Magazine of History and Biography*, LXX (October, 1962).

Certain battle reports that are germane to this study were found in the Cobb and McLaws papers, though of much greater assistance were Howell Cobb's Letter Books and Order Books, both in the University of Georgia Library, and, of course, *The War of the Rebellion: A Compilation of the Official Records of the Union and Confederate Armies*, 128 vols. (Washington, 1880-1901). Of some help was Robert U. Johnson and Clarence C. Buel, eds., *Battles and Leaders of the Civil War*, 4 vols. (New York, 1884-1887). Less valuable were battle reports published by the Confederate Congress in 1862 and 1864 and Allen D. Candler, ed., *Confederate Records of the State of Georgia*, 6 vols. (Atlanta, 1909-1910).

Newspapers that proved most useful were those of Milledgeville, particularly the *Federal Union*, which during part of the war was known as the *Confederate Union*, and of Athens, where the *Southern Banner*, long a Cobb organ, and the *Southern Watchman* were published. Limited use was made of the Augusta *Weekly Chronicle and Sentinel*, the Macon *Georgia Telegraph*, and the Atlanta *Confederacy*.

Numerous secondary works were consulted for specific as well as for background information. Among them were my *Howell Cobb's Confederate Career* (Tuscaloosa, 1959), for its treatment of the elder Cobb's military service, and E. Merton Coulter, *Lost Generation: The Life and Death of James Barrow, C.S.A.* (Tuscaloosa, 1956), for the information it contains on the Barrow family. Excellent for background were T. Conn Bryan's *Confederate Georgia* (Athens, 1953) and Bell I. Wiley's *The Life of Johnny Reb: The Common Soldier of the Confederacy* (Indianapolis, 1943). Because of its massive data on Confederate officers, Ezra J. Warner's *Generals in Gray* (Baton Rouge, 1959) provided valuable information on John B. Magruder, LaFayette McLaws, and others. Douglas Southall Freeman, *Lee's Lieutenants: A Study in Command*, 3 vols. (New York, 1942-1944), contains detailed information on the Peninsular and Maryland campaigns, in both of which John A. Cobb participated. Two works by T. Harry Williams, *Lincoln and His Generals* (New York, 1952) and *P. G. T. Beauregard: Napoleon in Gray* (Baton Rouge, 1954), were helpful for their information on military policies of both the Union and Confederate governments.

Index

DATE DUE

JUN 20 '73			
GAYLORD			PRINTED IN U.S.A.